THE
MAKING OF AMERICA
SERIES

PUTNEY

WORLD'S BEST KNOWN SMALL TOWN

David Plowden took this photo of one of the last steam engines to ride the Central Vermont tracks in November, 1956. The view across Kathan Meadows captures "The Newsboy" train headed south from Montreal to New London, Connecticut. Plowden, arguably the best-known photographer of trains and industrial design in the United States, lived in Putney as a youngster and attended The Putney School, where he got his start in photography.

THE
MAKING OF AMERICA
SERIES

PUTNEY
WORLD'S BEST KNOWN SMALL TOWN

PUTNEY HISTORICAL SOCIETY

ARCADIA
PUBLISHING

Copyright © 2003 by Putney Historical Society
ISBN 978-1-58973-162-2

Published by Arcadia Publishing
Charleston, South Carolina

For all general information contact Arcadia Publishing at:
Telephone 843-853-2070
Fax 843-853-0044
E-mail sales@arcadiapublishing.com
For customer service and orders:
Toll-Free 1-888-313-2665

Visit us on the Internet at www.arcadiapublishing.com

Front cover: *People gather around Putney Town Hall in 1953.*

CONTENTS

ACKNOWLEDGMENTS

The creation of this book has been quite a community accomplishment. The Putney Historical Society began planning for a new book almost seven years ago, hoping to continue the wonderful precedent set by the Fortnightly Club in 1953 when the first history was written. In a town where so many things have happened and so many people have contributed, it has been a challenge to select those events that make a lasting impression. Arcadia Publishing has eased the difficulty by establishing a framework within which we have operated. Using Arcadia's guidelines has helped us to select main ideas and some supporting details that give a sense of Putney, both in the world at large and in the daily pleasures that we enjoy by living in our small community. The beginning chapters about Putney's early development are presented as an overview. Further details can be found in many other publications listed in the bibliography, including the Fortnightly Club's history of 1953.

This book leaves numerous stories untold and emphasizes events rather than people. Because Putney has so many amazing people, the Historical Society will publish a *People of Putney, Volume II* within the next few years, once community volunteers have finished the interviewing processes now underway.

The effort to prepare this book was done in a grassroots manner. New research information was gathered by using primary resource documents and conducting interviews. First drafts were prepared from the information gathered and then Putney Public Library sponsored public critique sessions. From the public input, editors created a final manuscript. Once this was completed, facts that seemed untrue or misstated were double checked against the original research or verified with the people who shaped the events in question. Even so, as with all publications, there are probably a few errors. If you notice them, please tell us so we can "set the record straight."

Gathering photos was another community-wide effort. Over 60 people attended two library sponsored picture-gathering parties and contributed individual photos to our efforts. In addition, Bill and Ivy Darrow loaned photos from their collection of early twentieth century Putney. Marilyn Loomis and Laurel Ellis contributed photos from the Veterans Memorial collection. Marty Collins shared his collection of Judson Hall photographs. Ramona Lawrence, Dan Cassidy, David Rohn, Laura Heller, and George Soulos contributed photos from their personal albums. Finally, several professional photographers have given permission to use their photos. They include: Jim Powers from the Brattleboro Reformer, Jill Noss, Nic Block, Bob George, Jeremy Birch, Allan Seymour, Deborah Lazar, and David Plowden.

Funding for our community history project has been supported in part by the Vermont Council on the Humanities under a grant from the National Endowment for the Humanities and by the WEB Project under a grant from the Josephine Bay Paul and C. Michael Paul Foundation. In addition, Paul Levasseur and the Putney Public Library helped to increase our community outreach. We thank you all for your generous support!

Fern Tavalin coordinated the project. Primary writers included Laurel Ellis, Fern Tavalin, Stuart Strothman, and Stephen Anderson. Other contributing writers included Margot Torrey, Fred Breunig, Nancy Olson, Russell W. Ellis, Elizabeth Mills, Sue Mulcahy, Kevin Cutts, Patrick O'Brien, Hart Griffith, Vashon Townshend, Jan Thompson, Rosalyn Shaoul, Charles Dodge, Paul Gustafson, Carolyn Handy, Hannah Pick, Marion Daley, Betty Fedora, Ruth Barton, and Nancy Storrow.

Editorial assistance was provided by Steve Anderson, Elise Guyette, Tom Jamison, Lyssa Papazian, Paul and Karen Gustafson, Laura Heller, Jacquie Walker, Marilyn Loomis, Terri Ziter, Mary Lou Treat, Bob Treat, Jim Olivier, and many other participants during the two evenings of critique held at the Putney Cares Barn and the Putney Public Library.

Four Putney schools provided interviewing support: Laurie Fichter's eighth grade class at The Grammar School, Alan Owens's writing class at the Greenwood School, Stephen Sadlier's ESL-B students at The Putney School, and Landmark College students under guidance from Jan Thompson, Chris Grele, Tom Trenchard, Stuart Strothman, and Christina Nova.

Interviews were conducted in person or on the phone with the following people: Wayne Austin, Shirley Stockwell, Edith Rounds, Laurea Smead, Hugh Smead, Shirley Ellis, Donald Harlow, Julie Rosegrant, Judy Bagge, John Bagge, Ramona Lawrence, Nancy Stockwell, Lawrence Bryant, Carol Bryant, Paul Mousel, Glenn Davis, Jandira Handy, Phyllis Stromberg, Richard Stromberg, Justine Brewer, David Brewer, George Shumlin, Kitty Shumlin, Ellis Derrig, Rosalie Derrig, Harris Coomes, Laurence Wade, Beverly Stockwell, Floyd Ellis, Douglas Ellis, John Caldwell, Angeline Wood, Neil Quinn, James McCarthy, Jonathan Flaccus, Curtiss Tuff, Shirley Neathawk, Debra Fitzpatrick, Bert Wilkins, Daniel Hoviss, Honey Loring, John Smith, Rosemary Ladd, Matthew Broad, Mark Bateman, Jerry Baker, Dan Mitnik, Shari Gleidman, Saskia Whallon, Nancy Meyer, Indra Tracy, Lawrence Cook, Lynn Meyer, Thomas Hayes, Linn Bruce, Robin Burke, Jere Daniell, John Douglas, Jim McBean, Dennis Bailey, Toshiko Phipps, Ben Dow, Ines Zeller-Bass, Andrea and Evan Darrow, Ivy and Bill Darrow, Robert Goodell, Bob Rhodes, Barb and Richard Taylor, Jack Wallace, Shyla Irving, Randi Ziter, George Soulos, David and Janet Wells, Paul Grout, Harriet Rogers, Holton Wilson, Frank Wilson, Maryanne Saunders, Jonathan Flaccus, Andrea Scheidler, Ed Cassidy, Paul Wade, Louisa Amidon, Jonathan Altman, Calvin Farwell, Anita Coomes, George Mortimer, Malcolm Jones, Eva Mondon, Mal Herbert, and George and Laura Heller.

Finally, the significant support of three spouses throughout this project—namely Doug Ellis, Peter Tavalin, and Julie Strothman—deserves a very special thank you.

PREFACE

When measured against the thousands of years Putney sat untamed and undisturbed—except for the passing through of occasional native peoples—the last 250 years represent but a tiny fraction of its history. Yet the changes that have taken place in that brief span of time are astounding to consider. From raw wilderness, only accessible to the English settlements of 1753 by long, tedious, and dangerous journeys, Putney has developed to earn a distinguished place in the modern world.

The virgin trees that awaited the first inhabitants are now returned to the soil but some of their seedlings still stand silently witnessing the comings and goings of the succession of people who have called Putney home. Arrowheads turned up by plows on the Great Meadows—perhaps aimed at invading human targets—link the finder to the warrior or hunter who placed the point on his arrow at least a quarter millennium ago.

Especially in the spring, before new vegetation becomes the green camouflage of summer, many traces of Putney's history can still be seen scattered upon the landscape. Mysterious stone chambers conjure up images of truly ancient visitors. Largely buried piles of stones still mark the corners of some original lots of land assigned to the first proprietors. Cellar holes and stone walls silently reveal a glimpse of the toil and daily life of the pioneering settlers. The remnants of old dams and mill foundations along Sacketts and East Putney Brooks attest to the eras of growth and productivity that industrious men and women brought as they helped to shape a community in a place newly claimed from the wilderness. Sections of the pathways of abandoned roads and trails still wind through woods or follow streams to forgotten places.

Though typical of northern New England in its beginnings, the particular mix of people that came about as this town evolved is anything but typical. Diversity of opinion is a given, not a goal. Notable clashes between groups of citizens have been few since the Whigs and Tories, or Yorkers, settled their differences. In the nineteenth century it was the Perfectionists who roused the outrage of some of Putney's pious citizens; in the twentieth century it was the sudden influx of hippies. Things have not always progressed perfectly, but sooner or later life becomes harmonious again.

Today, even the slightly crooked way some buildings face Main Street is evidence that growth does not always occur as anticipated. The most significant catalyst of change in the essence of Putney since the mid-twentieth century has been the founding of several educational institutions that have gradually replaced farming and industry as the core of the town.

As we take our turn to carry on the business of life here, it is good to reflect on the legacy left by our predecessors. It is good to feel a connection to those who built our roads, lived in our homes, planted gardens in our soil, made decisions at Town Meeting, or just walked on the same paths where we walk.

We offer to the reader a description of what makes this town a place that makes long-term residents sacrifice better economic opportunities elsewhere to remain and increasingly draws new people to come and make their home here.

This photo taken by Nic Block in January of 2003 on the Westminster Road conveys the rural feeling that Putney has carried for over 200 years.

1. Blazing a Trail:
Early History to 1799

It is hard for the modern reader to imagine the rapid changes that the area now known as Putney underwent in the eighteenth century. Initially hunting and agricultural domain for the Western Abenaki, the land changed hands many times as British colonizers rivaled the French, Native Americans, and each other to stake their claims. At various times during the century, Putney came under the jurisdiction of Massachusetts, New Hampshire, and New York before legally affiliating with Windham County, Vermont. In the process, the land itself was transformed from thick forest to clear cut pasture.

Early Land Use and Dispute

Various bands of Western Abenaki lived along this section of the Connecticut River when the Europeans first came. According to oral tradition, native peoples began to inhabit the region just after the mountains and river valleys took their present shape. While only two ancient Native American archeological sites have been reported for Putney, other sites are probably present in the town and ample signs can be found nearby. In Bellows Falls faces etched in the bedrock (petroglyphs) may be seen just south of the bridge near the post office.

Several place names can be identified as native in origin or take their names from remains discovered onsite. The Connecticut River derives from "quonet-tu-cut" which means "long river with waves." Canoe Brook Road was so named because an abandoned canoe was found there. Other evidence of indigenous life is inferred from oral history and the habits acquired by the early English settlers. A sermon delivered by Reverend Elisha D. Andrews on Fast Day, April 8, 1825 recounted the following information about Abenaki life in Putney:

> The Great Meadows and the other intervals upon the river in this town was formerly inhabited by the aborigines of our country, as appears by the discovery of arrows, spears, axes, hoes, and broken pots. In several places on the intervals when the settlement of the whites began they found heaps of stones evidently brought by hand from the highlands and bearing

the marks of fire, and were supposed to constitute the fireplaces of the Indian wigwams. Stones of this description were found on the tract now occupied by Deacon Reynolds and his neighbors. But what were the names or numbers of the natives who occupied these grounds, I have been able to gain no information, nor can I say whether they had a permanent or only an occasional residence.

The first land survey on Putney soil was ordered by Massachusetts in the Fall of 1715 and included much of nearby Dummerston and Brattleboro. The crew included skilled surveyors, helpers, and Indians who were familiar with the area. The report begins, "The northeast corner boundary is the mouth of the brook, at the northward end of the Great Meadow. . . ." The eastern boundary of the parcel was the Connecticut River down to "about 3 miles southward of the West River." For much of the way the surveyors followed an Indian path along the Connecticut, the same path that Reverend John Williams and more than 100 others were made to travel after being taken captive by French soldiers and Indians in Deerfield a decade earlier.

The surveyor's job was to mark off 44,000 acres, or 15 square miles, of land, as one part of the settlement of a boundary dispute between Connecticut and Massachusetts. Agreeable to the findings of a joint committee, Massachusetts would let Connecticut have the land, but it would remain part of Massachusetts and under its jurisdiction. Connecticut then decided to sell its "Equivalent Lands" at an auction to take place in April

For many years the Putney Historical Society Museum displayed the remains of what is thought to have been old Abenaki bones. Shaman Pee Mee performed a ceremony of re-burial near the Great Meadows in 1981.

A monument to the second Putney fort was placed on site at the Great Meadows and moved to higher ground in 1936 to protect it from floods.

1716. Five Harvard graduates from the Boston area bought the parcel above Northfield as an investment. William Brattle, John White, and Anthony Stoddard each bought a share, and Jeremiah Dummer and William Dummer bought one share together.

Massachusetts's northern boundary with New Hampshire was even more uncertain than its southern one with Connecticut. Massachusetts assumed all this land in the wilderness above Northfield was within its borders and kept pushing the boundary northward, leading to disputes with New Hampshire. By 1736 Massachusetts had chartered towns from Northfield up to "Number 4" (now Charlestown, New Hampshire), but no towns were chartered within the Equivalent Lands because that was already owned by private individuals. By 1740 New Hampshire had won the boundary game, and the King of England decreed that the line should be where it is today.

The Putney parcel included land at the Great Meadows, which held an abundance of majestic pines more than 100 feet high and tall enough to make masts for the King's ships. Hearing of the great timber wealth, 70 Englishmen came in 1733 to cut timber and float the logs down the river to merchants in New London, Connecticut. Soon after, on September 12, 1734, Ompawmet presented a land claim for the Great Meadows to the English at Fort Dummer. A note in the Acts and Resolves of the Province of Massachusetts records the following transaction: "Ordered 120 pounds to John Stoddard, Esq. and Captain Israel Williams to be by them paid and delivered to Ompawmet Indian upon executing before as many Indian witnesses as may be, a deed of conveyance of his right and title (of the Great Meadow, part of the Equivalent Land.)"

Settlers built Putney's first fort by 1740 in the clearing on the Great Meadows, with 10 men sent to accompany them for the purposes of scouting and guarding. This fort and others like it served as outpost stations for British exploration, conquest, and colonization of the Connecticut River Valley. Deerfield, Massachusetts provided their base of operation. One recorded incident in the English-French wars concerning William Phipps, an early settler, appears in several histories and tells a dramatic story that took place on July 5, 1745. Phipps was at work hoeing corn on the Great Meadow when two Abenaki in French employ sprang upon him and dragged him to the woods nearby. There, after a short parley, one of the Abenaki departed, leaving Phipps under the care of his comrade. Phipps, watching for an opportunity to escape, struck his keeper down with his hoe and seizing his gun, gave the other, who was returning, a fatal wound. Phipps tried to run back to the fort, but before he could reach it three other Abenaki captured and killed him.

On October 11 of that same year, French soldiers and Abenaki from Canada attacked the fort again. An English witness said that about 50 of the enemy assaulted the fort. The attackers were in the meadow scarcely over an hour, but captured Nehemiah Howe and carried him to Canada where he died two years later. They also killed and scalped David Rugg, who was coming down the river in a canoe. Robert Baker, his companion, was able to reach the opposite shore and escaped.

Not much damage was done to the fort in the attack, but the Abenaki drove away and killed all the cattle, carrying away with them the best part of the flesh and hides. After this, Colonel Josiah Willard (1693–1750), who was in command at nearby Fort Dummer, started out with a group of men after them, but being unable to catch up with them, gave up and returned. These incidents forced people to flee to safer places for protection and thus the fort was abandoned. The records do not say with certainty what happened to the fort, whether it was destroyed by whites before leaving, assaulted and burned by Abenakis, or whether it simply fell into decay.

TOWN CHARTERS

The issuance of town charters in the early to mid-eighteenth century was a politically conscious move by the governor of New Hampshire to establish claims in the western territories of what is present-day Southeastern Vermont. Since there was no need to use the land for pioneer expansion at that time there was not much of an expectation that the land would be settled in the short run. However, the creation of charters did establish a priority to the order of eventual settlement. While the pace of moving north was certainly affected by the threat of Abenaki and French attacks, the other equally significant contributing factor to the timing of settlement was the massive overpopulation of Connecticut.

Josiah Willard (1716–1796), son of the colonel mentioned previously, led a petition for a Putney charter and on December 26, 1753, the town received its first charter, issued by Governor Benning Wentworth of the New Hampshire Grants under King George II of England. The New Hampshire charter gave the grantees of Putney, many of whom were heirs of the original owners, an area approximately 5 1/2 miles square, enclosing 19,360 acres. This was to be divided into 56 shares apportioned to 44 grantees, including two women, plus shares for the king, the governor, and the church (glebe land). As elsewhere in New England, many of the proprietors, to whom the town was granted, acted as land speculators with no intention of settling in Putney. These original proprietors were ready to sell their lots to others who were eager to buy land and establish homes for their families.

Within five years, according to the charter stipulations, each grantee or his heirs had to plant and cultivate 5 acres per 50 acres owned. All pine trees fit for masts for the Royal Navy were to be preserved for that use and not cut without royal license. Besides the duties imposed upon them in the charter, proprietors had the legal responsibility of determining the actual settlement and development of the town. This included laying out roads, providing for saw mills and grist mills, providing a minister and a church, attracting such artisans as blacksmiths and carpenters, and providing for education and military training. As soon as the town grew to 50 families, settlers also had "the liberty of holding two fairs, one of which shall be held on the second Thursday in September" and which were not to continue longer than the following Saturday. Town Meeting was set for the first Monday of March every year.

The struggle for territory between France and Great Britain prevented fulfillment of the initial charter responsibilities for over a decade. To protect themselves, settlers from Putney, joined by those across the river in Westmoreland, New Hampshire, built a second fort at the Great Meadows in 1755. They remained near to its confines until about 1760, just after the British victory in Quebec City on the Plains of Abraham in 1759.

In 1761 the proprietors met at Josiah Willard's house in Wincester, New Hampshire to discuss the town layout. The plan shows that a rocky ridge just west of Banning Road (formerly named Glebe Road) was chosen for the 600 acres required for the Church of England and The Society for the Propagation of the Gospel. Eight hundred bumpy acres along East Putney Brook (formerly named Shaws Brook) were reserved for Governor Wentworth and the Great Meadows went to Josiah Willard himself. Fifty acres on the eastern slope of Bare Hill were set aside for a town center or for public use. Lots were reserved for mills along East Putney and Sacketts Brook. A 6 rod (99 foot) wide strip through each lot was reserved as allowance for highway use. Lot boundaries were demarcated with heaps of stones piled in each corner.

Before the proprietors could implement their new plan, colonial governance switched by royal proclamation in 1765 from New Hampshire to New York. Josiah Willard led the request and Governor Moore of the Province of New York issued a confirmatory charter on November 6, 1766 under King George III. With these 13 intervening years, the names of only four of the original grantees reappeared in the confirmatory charter.

The second charter paralleled the first, with a few new requirements. One lot of land had to be set aside for the public school master and one lot for the first minister. Town Meeting was to be held in the most public place on the second Tuesday in May, and one family for each 1,000 acres had to settle in the town within three years. Settlers came mainly from Massachusetts and Connecticut, usually purchasing their lots sight unseen. By 1770 Putney had attracted 50 families, yielding a town population of approximately 300. That year, eligible male voters held the first Town Meeting in Putney, Cumberland County, Province of New York.

With the change in governance, many former New Hampshire inhabitants became New York adherents (or Yorkers), especially in the southeastern towns of the original New Hampshire grants, while others remained loyal to New Hampshire or sought freedom from both. Since many Yorkers were Tory minded, meaning they supported the king, issues quickly extended from local politics to national, especially as the relations between Great Britain and the American colonies worsened.

AMERICAN INDEPENDENCE AND VERMONT STATEHOOD

The move toward American Independence and Vermont statehood was not an easy path for Putney residents. The Fortnightly history of Putney vividly retells this period of colonial history and is replete with fascinating details. Briefly summarized, in 1766 and 1768 New York established the county of Cumberland so that the New Hampshire Grants could have New York courts, judges, and other officers closer to them than Albany. In 1768 Joseph Lord of Putney was appointed Second Judge to serve the Inferior Court of Common Pleas. On May 8, 1770, Putney organized as a town and elected its first town officials, including Noah Sabin as town clerk. In 1772 Noah Sabin was appointed as a county court judge to assist Lord in his duties. With this appointment, Putney town government was formally connected to Yorker interests.

Outbreaks of violence occurred around Putney as citizens attempted to prevent New York courts or officials from carrying out their duties, especially as they related to collecting money for additional land payments to New York (payments to New

Many of the original English settlers are buried in the Old North Cemetery, located on the Westminster Road.

Hampshire already having been made) under threat of foreclosure and debtors' prison. With citizens supporting both sides, tension rose. On March 13, 1775, the feeling against the Yorker courts became so strong that a number of opposers, including several from Putney, attempted to prevent the New York court from holding session in Westminster. Violence ensued, leading to two deaths. This attempt became known as the Westminster Massacre. As a result of the massacre, Noah Sabin was arrested, sent to New York for trial, and not returned to his home in Putney until a year later.

As war with Great Britain neared, disputes over which militia to join made matters even worse. In 1775 the Continental Congress commanded New York to raise an army of 3,000. New York in turn required Cumberland County to furnish 125 men. The anti-Yorker element in Putney Town Meeting sent a protest to the Westminster Convention where the Yorker officers of Cumberland County were being chosen. Rather than fight as part of an army from New York, they wanted independence. In a counter move, James Clay of Putney held meetings to arouse opposition to the creation of an independent state. He was arrested on August 10, 1775, kept in jail for six days, and then returned to Putney.

As soon as the 13 colonies proclaimed independence from Great Britain in 1776, leaders of independence for the New Hampshire Grants petitioned the Continental Congress for admission to the Union. Blocked by land claims from New York, the request was denied. An angry group of New Hampshire Grants men gathered in Westminster in January of

Cub Scout Duncan Momaney and his dad Michael pause during one of several efforts to clear and preserve the Kathan Cemetery, most likely the site of the first formal burial (Judith Bellows Moore, 1756) in Putney.

1777 and proclaimed themselves the state of New Connecticut. In July they met again in Windsor to write a constitution and officially declared themselves the independent republic of Vermont.

By some counts in 1778 there were 480 Yorker sympathizers in nine towns in the vicinity of Putney. Of the voting males aged 16 and above, Putney had 69 for New York and 26 against. The Putney Selectmen's records of the May Town Meeting record that Captain James Clay and Deacon Samuel Minott were chosen "to meet with Hinsdale, Brattleborough, Westminster and Rockingham and any other town committees to consult for the good of the State of New York against the pretended State of Vermont."

In 1779 the new Republic of Vermont established a militia. The new republic also passed a law allowing Vermont officers to take possession of lands and personal property of those who were still adhering to the King of England. In establishing this militia each town was to classify men and furnish them as the need arose. Men who refused to serve were fined or their possessions taken away. In April 1779, Captain James Clay, Lieutenant Benjamin Wilson, and a Mr. Cummings all refused to be drafted into the Vermont militia. They refused also to pay a fine, or the cost of a substitute, whereupon Sergeant McWain seized two cows belonging to Clay and Wilson, planning to sell them a week hence. Other Yorker sympathizers from Putney and other towns, under the leadership of Colonel Patterson, arrived upon the scene, stole the cows from McWain, and returned them to their owners. McWain sent in a complaint to Governor Chittenden about this, and Ethan Allen was ordered by the governor to proceed to Putney to assist the sheriff with these Yorkers.

Ethan Allen arrived in Putney on May 24. Forthwith the Yorkers wrote the following note to Governor Clinton of New York:

> The committee of this (Cumberland) county who are now met for the purpose of opposing the authority of the state of Vermont take this opportunity to inform, your excellency by Express that Col. Ethan Alline (Allen) with a number of Green Mt. Boys made his appearance in the county yesterday well armed and equipt for the purpose of reducing the loyal inhabitants of this county to submission to the authority of the State of Vermont and made prisoners of Col. Eleazar Patterson, Lieut. Col. (John) Sergeant and all the militia officers except one in Brattleborough. . . . Col. Alline asserted he had 500 with him . . . Col Alline treated the people here with the most insulting language, assaulted and wounded several persons with his sword without the least provocation, and bids defiance to the State of New York. . . . Our situation here is truly critical and distressing and we most humbly beseech your excellency to take the most . . . efficient measures for our relief: otherwise our Persons and Property must be at the disposal of Ethan Allen, which is more to be dreaded than Death with all its Terrors.
>
> Samuel Minott, chairman
> Putney, Vermont

17

On the day that 36 of these arrested men were in Westminster at court, Allen arrived there. He was allowed to speak as a citizen and harangued the court with "words of fire" because some of the prisoners had been discharged before trial by reason of homage or lack of evidence. In the final judgment, 14 Putney men were convicted.

As a result, on June 2, the Vermont legislature enacted a law declaring that all persons in the state were forbidden to hold any office except a Vermont office. To establish unity, on June 3, 1779, Governor Chittenden issued a proclamation of pardon to all rioters and persons who had at any time opposed the Republic of Vermont in mistaken allegiance to New York.

Despite these actions, the town of Putney maintained a New York system of governance. In 1778 the town voted to set up a whipping post and stocks. In 1779 and 1780 the town held two Town Meetings, a March meeting for Vermont and a May meeting for New York, with two town clerks, two sets of constables, and so forth.

Yorker sentiment was still so strong in Putney in 1780 that the opposition appeared in force at May Town Meeting and put an end to all voting. In June of 1780, 13 Yorkers and 26 Whigs of Putney were drafted into the Vermont militia. In that same year Governor Chittenden came to Putney to talk with the Yorkers to hear their grievances and ask why they continued to adhere to New York principles. Even after the encounter with Governor Chittenden, the Yorkers kept on meeting and asserting allegiance to New York. However, from 1781 on, Putney was officially part of Windham County, Vermont.

The Revolutionary War ended in 1783 with the Treaty of Paris and hopes of Vermont statehood strengthened. By 1784 many Yorkers were gradually submitting to the laws of Vermont; others petitioned the republic for the privilege of taking the oath of allegiance. By 1786 New York and Vermont were beginning to settle their difficulties, and many of the faithful Yorkers were being recompensed by New York with either money or land. However, New York continued to block another Vermont request to join the Union in 1787.

By 1789 Kentucky was asking for admission to the United States as a slave state. To keep a slave state/free state balance, the northern states placed pressure on New York to settle its land claim. New York finally passed a law giving a "certain area within its confine" (meaning Vermont), permission to become a state. On October 7, 1790, Vermont received this "permission" to join the Union. Along with the privileges of statehood, Vermont had to pay New York $30,000 for all rights and titles to New York land claims. In 1791 Vermont became the fourteenth state.

By the time of statehood, Putney's population had escalated from its original 300 in 1770 to nearly 2,000. It never developed the village center as envisioned by its first town planners, set aside on Bare Hill. Rather, settlers built on the lots they had purchased, scattering their homes and farms throughout the township and along the few roads and turnpikes. They established 12 school districts, close enough for neighborhood children to walk to school. Many of these small villages within the town also housed conveniently located taverns, stores, and churches. Within less than 60 years of the initial British settlements in Putney, the huge tracts of forest that greeted the first settlers had been cut clear. As the century came to a close, the population declined slightly from its peak of 1,848 in 1791 to 1,574. A few of the family clusters began to disappear, leaving homes on the highest elevations without year-round inhabitants, especially on Putney Mountain where the thin soil depleted quickly. Despite the vacated homesteads, farmers who lived at lower elevations continued to use the land as summer pastures.

Charles Kathan built this house in the late 1780s for his family of 10 children. In 1839 the dwelling became one of the three main communal residences occupied by the Perfectionists until their departure in 1847. The house was eventually torn down to make room for the Post Office, which opened in 1963.

2. Shaping a Town: 1800–1899

For the first 50 years of the nineteenth century, Putney had a fairly stable population of about 1,500 farmers, small business owners, and small-scale manufacturers. Land speculation led to an accumulation of capital, transients provided a labor pool for farm and factory, and agricultural experimentation meant better breeding of sheep and cows. A unique interpretation of the Revivalists' teachings of the early to mid-1800s led to Putney's first clash with a counter-culture. As the century moved on, Putney supplied soldiers and funds to support the Union Army during the Civil War. By the end of the century, the town's population had slowly declined as inhabitants moved west, giving up the rigors of life on isolated hill farms for more fertile pastures.

Development of a Mill Town

By the beginning of the nineteenth century, timber was scarce. Reverend Elisha Andrews referred to the shortages when he delivered his 1825 sermon about the early history of Putney:

> . . . our forests have so far disappeared as to have but a moderate supply of fuel and even a deficiency of valuable timber. The pine has become so scarce as to be almost a curiosity, few farms have more than a necessary supply for the repair of buildings, and most farms have none at all. So, we are dependent on the country east and north of us for our materials for building.

The open pastures and flowing streams gave rise to sheep and dairy farming, the growth of tobacco and corn, and the development of many small-scale industries that would ebb and flow over the next two centuries. The frenzied rush for land that hit Putney, as well as many other Vermont towns, slowed and the town's population stabilized to an average of 1,500 people from 1800 to 1850. Most Vermont towns lost population to an early westward expansion into the frontier territories of New York state. Some of these pioneers, prompted by new federal laws allowing people to settle/conquer lands west of the Appalachians, moved even further. Although this has been

The Lower Mill, or Owl Mill, was built in 1828 by the Robertsons, but destroyed by a freshet the same year. Rebuilt within the year, this version was destroyed by fire in 1903 and rebuilt once again.

described as a statewide trend, Putney's development may have followed a slightly different path.

While conducting research in 1980, former Putney Historical Society president Nancy Calicchio uncovered information about 1800–1820 migration and immigration patterns of Putney that contradict long held myths about the town's past. Calicchio tested the theory that Putney began as a farming town that lost its farms as residents moved west. Her analysis of census records and land sales of Putney from 1800 to 1820 shows a town in great flux with only 40 percent of the population appearing on two consecutive census counts. The majority of those who came and went were poor, recent immigrants to the town. Slightly over half of the newcomers owned property and two-thirds owned no house. Of those who did own land, most held less than 15 acres. Most stayed just a few years, living in boarding houses or log cabins. They supplied a source of day labor, did not accumulate assets, and started from scratch again when they emigrated to nearby towns like Dummerston, Grafton, Brattleboro, and Westminster. Calicchio identified only five families that left town and headed west to New York or Ohio.

Those who stayed were not primarily farmers. Only a small portion fit the description of the typical farmer with a secondary occupation. The vast majority lived on the exchange of goods and services. They were tradespeople who farmed a little, rather than farmers who traded a little. A partial list of small businesses in 1810 shows the diversity of economic activity. At that time, Putney residents operated six sawmills, four grist mills, one carding

21

mill, two fulling mills, one brick yard, one slate quarry, two tanneries, at least two inns, and five stores. Three people were engaged in a major way in the buying and selling of land. In addition, a lot of professional people lived in town, especially for the size of the population. These included three lawyers, four doctors, and two ministers.

A lot of money changed hands due to people coming and leaving. Land brokers such as Phineas White, Theophilus Crawford, and Thomas Green bought up the land of the people moving out and resold it to some of those moving in. In doing so, the speculators accumulated quite a bit of money and created the financial circumstances to establish a larger scale industry. The migrant population provided a changing base for the accumulation of capital among some of the resident families and land speculators. As a small group hung on and a large group circled around them, coming and going, Putney acquired the labor force and capital necessary to start a big mill.

In 1818 or 1819, Solomon Stimson, Lawson Green, and Ebenezer Fairbanks built the first Putney paper mill. To the 1820 census enumerator, the owners reported an employment of four men, three women, and two boys with an output of 2,425 reams, valued at $5,000. By the end of the first year of production, the new owners found themselves overextended by the costs of setting up a viable business. In financial jeopardy, they executed a mortgage with Jonathan Knight, Phineas White, and Benjamin Smith. The Vermont General Assembly passed a legislative act to defer all civil suits against the paper mill so that they might stay out of debtor's prison and pay off their debt. Even so, the original partners sold their business in 1825 to George Robertson from Scotland who went into business with his brother William and applied the knowledge he had gained from the Scottish paper making industry. Thus began the town's dominant industry, one that both peaked in production and fell into bankruptcy many times over in the ensuing years.

Reverend Andrews alluded to the constant shift in population in 1825, lamenting:

> How little do most of us know of those who lived here half a century ago. Their names in many instances have gone to oblivion together with their characteristic feelings and desires and very soon the places that know us will know us no more. This century will not terminate before most of us will be forgotten and a race of new beings will occupy our places and dwell in our habitations.

Ironically, Reverend Andrews himself was to move within a decade of giving his 1825 sermon. Once relocated in Michigan, he corresponded frequently with David Crawford, a wealthy farmer and businessman whose 1840s home was located at 105 Westminster Road. What remains of their letters from 1837 to 1851 gives modern readers a glimpse into the economic and social climate of Putney at that time.

In June 1842, Crawford described the changing character of the town and its implications for "the Street" (the area of Westminster West Road near Putney Central School) where many of the earliest dwellings in Putney were erected.

Because spiritual life was central in defining New England town centers, the Congregational Church secured the village's position as a center.

This photo of Putney taken around 1889 shows the development of a bona-fide village center, complete with businesses, homes, mills, and a church.

Changes in the location of business have taken place since you were here. All the stores and nearly all the mechanics are now down at the Village, as we call it. Several new handsome houses have been built there and the whole Village much improved. Our old Meeting house required repairs and none below Judge White would contribute to it. The Methodists were talking about building a new house at the Village, in which nearly all these would have joined, unless we would build there. Had the Methodists built the first house, it would have received our Congregation. Under these circumstances . . . [we] deemed it best to take down the old house and build a new one. We have erected a very pretty house about opposite Mr. Grouts store. . . . The Methodists are building a Meeting house on the site of the old Hatter's shop near Perry's Tavern.

The temperance cause has made great advance in this place as well as abroad. We have had two stores which sold spirit until last fall when the cause of temperance was taken up by drinkers. Temperance men aided and encouraged and the work went forward—funds were raised and everything spiritous at the stores was purchased. That which was fit to be used medicinally was placed in the care of the physician and the remainder destroyed. We have two taverns which sell it, but their sales are curtailed. A number of "hard cases" were reclaimed.

Once settlers began to use the water power created by the falls on the Sacketts Brook, the cluster of businesses in that area grew steadily as did housing lots. Construction of

Methodist and Congregational churches made the shift complete. This shift in town center from the agricultural region of the Street to the production and manufacturing region of the Village emphasized the importance of the mill-based activities as the town shifted to a mixed economy of farming and small-scale production.

THE ECONOMICS OF AGRICULTURE

The Crawford-Andrews letters were filled with references to buying and selling property and securing loans as the two discussed their business strategies for land speculation and commodities brokering. Particularly interesting to Putney's history are Crawford's accounts of raising sheep so that wool could be sold to local and regional markets for the production of cloth. The introduction of Merino sheep to Weathersfield Bow by William Jarvis in 1811 began Vermont's reputation for producing fine wool and later for sheep breeding. The hilly terrain, which was better suited to sheep grazing than grain production, enhanced the emphasis on sheep. The federal tariff on woolens passed in 1824 gave local producers a competitive advantage in the marketplace that would last for more than two decades.

Talk of lifting tariffs and other forms of regulation gave rise to general concerns about government policy. In reference to the price of wool, Crawford told Andrews in September 1845, "I doubt whether [the price of wool] will rise while the Tariff question is unsettled. Manufacturers have not confidence in the stability of the measures of Government and the labor of Country suffers for the benefit of Demagoguery."

Sheep farming stayed popular in Putney until the end of the nineteenth century. This photo shows an unidentified flock in East Putney.

24

By January 1846 their correspondence shifted from discussions about tariffs to the price and quality of wool. Andrews shipped his raw wool from Michigan to Crawford for sale in New England markets. The wool arrived late in season, injured in looks from bagging and transport, and labeled "smutty" by a potential buyer. Crawford had a difficult time selling Andrews's product at a reasonable price. In lieu of payment, James Keyes of the Putney Woolen Mill offered to process Andrews's next sheep clip in exchange for half of the cloth it yielded.

David Crawford was one of the early, successful sheep breeders in the country. The Crawford farms yielded 6 pounds of wool per sheep decades before this became the norm. Difficulty in the sale of his partner's wool prompted Crawford to discuss the quality of his livestock and why it brought a higher price:

> I think I have a more profitable kind of sheep than yours. We have taken pains to improve the breed so as to get longer fleeces and still preserve the quality of the wool. I sold 397 fleeces which weighed 1,393 pounds. As it is here no object to raise lambs for sale unless they are superior I raise only from my best Ewes. I make the selection at shearing time. I direct my shearers when they think they have an Ewe with fine wool and heavy fleece to put her into a stable by herself till I can weigh the fleece. At last shearing I adopted the rule that if it weighed 3 1/2 or over, I put a mark upon the sheep. In this way I marked between 80 and 90 Ewes whose fleeces weighed from 3 1/2 to 5 pounds. From them I expect lambs—wool fine, long, thick on the skin. . . .

Anticipation that Congress might lift the 1824 tariff brought instability to the production and manufacturing of wool in New England. "The feeling of certainty that the tariff will work badly for the woollen [sic] business has reduced the price of wool low and very few sales [are made]. Manufacturers buy but little, or no faster than they work it. . . . None in Putney will bring over 30 cts." Repeal of the tariff in 1846 put the wool industry on the decline and the development of railroads placed Vermont in direct competition with western farmers who were able to take advantage of the vast amounts of cheap land in the west to establish large sheep operations. The ensuing price competition made it difficult for marginal businesses and farmers to sustain their endeavors. Crawford ended his September 1846 letter by saying, "If you should send your wool [I] will cheerfully attend to anything in regard to it you may desire. But I know of nothing which can be done with wool at present which seems to promise well." While the growth and manufacturing of wool in Vermont slowly declined in the following decades, Crawford was able to see several high priced seasons, despite his gloomy predictions.

THE PUTNEY PERFECTIONISTS

The letters between Crawford and Andrews shifted in tone and content in November of 1847 and June of 1848 as they discussed the activities of John Humphrey Noyes Jr. and the Perfectionists. Andrews used his preacher's fire to write:

My heart bled when I heard the sad disclosures which your letter made. Yet they were not altogether unexpected, for I repeatedly predicted such a result when at Putney. I did it not from any facts in the case that would lead to such a conclusion, but from that I have never known any cases of pretended immediate revelation from heaven but what ended in the same lamentable manner, down right licentiousness.

After graduating from Dartmouth College at the age of 19, John Humphrey Noyes Jr. studied law for about a year. In August 1831, he made a profession of religion and became a member of the Congregational Church in Putney. After studying a year at the Theological Seminary at Andover, Massachusetts and a year at the Theological Seminary connected with Yale College, Noyes received a license to preach in August of 1833. Influenced by the ideas of Perfectionism that were circulating around New Haven, Connecticut at the time, Noyes declared himself a Perfectionist in February 1834. In response, Yale withdrew his license. Later, Noyes was also excommunicated from the Putney Congregational Church.

While it is often thought that Noyes began Perfectionism, the doctrine of Christian Perfection had already been taught by a number of revival leaders including James Latourette, John B. Foot, and Hiram Shelton. The Perfectionists held that Christ had actually returned to earth before the close of the Apostolic Age, and that his work of saving men from sin was complete. The ordinances of baptism and communion were done away with, the Sabbath abolished, and the whole moral law as contained in the Ten Commandments annulled.

Noyes determined to establish a "Bible family" in which all should be perfectly equal, worldly goods should be held in common, and those who were married should renounce their traditional marriage ties in favor of a "complex marriage." He and his associates formally renounced their allegiance to the United States and set up house in "celestial order." John Humphrey Noyes's views were expressed in the *Perfectionist*, a paper published on the first and fifteenth of each month from 1843 to 1846 and sold for $1 a year. This succeeded an earlier publication called *The Witness*.

To local preachers, Noyes's practices desecrated the holy Sabbath. Reverend Hubbard Eastman, who spent hundreds of pages describing their revolting behavior, used examples that seem innocent by today's standards:

> On Sunday afternoon, Noyes and his followers had no meetings in their chapel but instead spent time, after the manner of a holiday, in rambling over the field, or riding about town—to the annoyance of the sober citizens—in their pleasure carriages; —the *nobility* occupying the best vehicles, and the lower class those of a secondary order.... In the evening, after a great supper, they spent the time in conversing upon what they called *religious* subjects. What consummate hypocrisy! —fiddling, dancing, *card-playing*, etc., in short any gaming or amusements which the spirit that was among *them* inclined them to follow.

The Perfectionists, also known as "Communists" and "Free-Lovers," enjoyed apparent prosperity for a few years. When the details of the "family" system went from theory to action, however, the people of Putney rose in indignation. In 1847 Noyes was arrested for the high misdemeanor of adultery and bonded to appear for trial at the superior court. Upon release he immediately left the state, forfeiting his bail bond. The property holdings of the group were significant as follower John R. Miller wrote in December 1851:

> It is generally supposed that we have sold out our property in Putney and have entirely abandoned the town. This is not so, but quite the contrary. We still own a good farm of 200 acres which cost $7,000; six dwelling houses, a store, chapel, printing office and a grist mill, besides other property; making in all not less than $15,000.

The Putney Perfectionist community eventually fell apart, losing the successful businesses it had operated including a grist mill, print shop, and general store. A portion of the Putney family joined other Perfectionists in upstate New York. Noyes himself went on to lead America's first communal society—the Oneida Community.

Whether the deleterious influence of the doctrine and practices of the sect remained in the Putney community for a long time is up for question. But two of the three main houses the Perfectionists inhabited still stand. Built by Noyes and his new wife in 1838, the house at 9 Cul-de-sac (off Christian Square) was later used as a dwelling for a group of Perfectionists. The large building, demolished for construction of the current Post

Locust Grove on "The Street" was the family home of John Noyes and later of his son John Humphrey Noyes. The barn in this photo was converted to a home by the Sprague family in 1971. The homestead (out of view) is now Putney Cares.

This group photo of Civil War veterans from the Colonel Greenwood Post No. 90 of the Grand Army of the Republic was taken on a Memorial Day in the late 1800s.

Office, was the group's second major dwelling. John Noyes Sr.'s home, called "Locust Grove" (now the residence building for Putney Cares) was the third communal dwelling. A historical marker outside the building commemorates its famous former owner. The Perfectionist Chapel is still standing on Main Street and currently houses the Putney Diner, although the large front pillars and overhang, once part of the façade, have long since disappeared.

THE LATER NINETEENTH CENTURY

When the flurry of agitation and rumor-mongering against the Perfectionists abated with their departure, Putney entered the relatively quiet decade of the 1850s. However, increasing political clashes between North and South soon disturbed daily life once again. By 1861 the Civil War hit Putney in much the same way it did other Vermont towns. State response to federal calls for enlistment placed quotas on towns that were easy to fulfill at first, but difficult to meet as the war raged on. Even though war taxes placed a strain on the budget, Town Meeting articles were passed to ensure local volunteers that the town would cover $7 per month for the required nine months of service in the event that the state did not make its payment to the volunteer. Some generous articles that were passed were also rescinded though, as in the case of a Mrs. Elliot, whose son Charles died at Andersonville prison. On March 4, 1867 voters approved a payment to her of $400 only to have it reconsidered and voted down at a special Town Meeting on April 5, 1867.

28

Putney enlistees served in all the major battles of the war and many were wounded, losing limbs and suffering gunshot injuries to the hips, thighs, legs, and arms that would last the rest of their lives. The *Personal War Sketches* of the Colonel W.H. Greenwood Post Number 90 of the Putney Grand Army of the Republic lists volunteers who fought at the First and Second Battle of Bull Run, Antietam, Spotsylvania, Charleston, Fredericksburg, and the famous Pickett's Charge at Gettysburg. Some were even part of the guard detail that led 3,000 prisoners from the Gettysburg battlefield down to Baltimore.

The experience of Patrick Mooney tells a typical tale. Patrick was born in Ireland in 1822 and entered the Union service in 1863 as a private. On June 23, 1864 he was taken prisoner at Petersburg, Virginia and confined in Andersonville and Libby prisons until his final release. The *Personal War Sketches* records that Mooney "suffered the horrible tortures that only the inmates of these prisons can ever know." When the Civil War ended in Northern victory the fortunate soldiers returned to their families while the unfortunate ones were buried in Putney cemeteries or left in unmarked Southern graves. A Union flag that covered the coffin of one local soldier is still on display at the Putney Historical Society.

After the Civil War, the population of Putney slowly declined as people left the hilltop farms in favor of town life or westward migration. The main centers in Putney village and East Putney remained active with small businesses, mills, machine shops, and farms along the Connecticut River. Railroads opened Putney to the far reaches of the world when they came through in 1850, a convenience that would last for more than 100 years. Via train, local merchants shipped paper, wool, tobacco, apples, milk, and ice as well as many other products to distant regional markets such as Boston. Iced railroad cars allowed for the shipment of butter and cheese to city markets. While the economy of the two villages continued, homes and farms in more distant sections of town were abandoned, especially in the area of Putney Mountain where the soil was especially thin and the climate harsh. Sheep farming, having increased slightly due to the demand for wool for the production of Civil War uniforms, fell to half the level it once had been.

Despite a falling population and a marginal economy, a few Putney residents developed some innovative business ideas. Charles Houghton is one such example. The Houghton farm was situated in Lot #10 of the original *Proprietor's Book* and sold to the Houghtons in 1792 by Peter Stuyvesant of New York. The farm and main house passed through several generations. When Charles Stuart Houghton died in 1859 he left his prosperous estate to his wife Hannah Perry. In 1865 Hannah deeded the farm to her son Charles, although she continued to live there.

Charles, a 43-year-old Boston lawyer, established a small herd of registered Holstein cattle on the Putney farm in 1866, the first such herd in Vermont and the second in the country. He and William Cheney of Massachusetts, a pioneer importer of the breed, started a Holstein breeders association in 1870 that, along with another group, began the Holstein-Friesian Association. Charles was the first secretary and treasurer of the organization and much of the early business was conducted out of his Putney homestead. Many interested people frequented the farm, and the volume of mail generated by the breeders' association through the Putney post office boosted the town's status up to third class. This improved postal designation meant that the town acquired a postmaster, appointed in 1903 by President

Theodore Roosevelt. Charles's son Frederick continued the family tradition and eventually became president of the Holstein-Friesian Association. From his Putney homestead, Frederick began the *Holstein-Friesian Register*, a journal with a circulation of 5,000.

While wealthy families like the Houghtons amassed land (at Frederick's death the farm contained 900 acres) and prospered from farm-related businesses, others lived at subsistence level. At age 88, Justin Homer Bacon (1873–1970) described early life on the Bacon family farm, located near the top of West Hill, in a manuscript he entitled *Notes to Posterity*. His account relays a vivid image of the property and shows the solitude and isolation of those few remaining farmsteads far away from the village center:

> The old farm where I spent my first years (nearly eight) has left very many deep impressions. It comprised 3 tillage fields, 2 orchards, a sugar lot, 4 pastures, two of which did not adjoin the farm directly, a wood lot, and was well watered by 4 brooks. Drinking water came from a fine spring but as the pipe ran over an intervening hill it had to be filled with water by a hand pump so that it would siphon the supply to the big cistern in the back room and to the water tub in the barnyard. The supply was ample and pumping was rarely needed. There was almost no level land. It was decidedly a hill farm, sloping mostly to the east, the house being located near the middle of the long slope. . . .
>
> Much of what I learned was in the house. . . . Inside, the house had a small south entry, a large kitchen which served as dining room and general work room presided over by the big grandfather clock, a sitting room heated by a sheet iron chunk stove, in the windows of which were many house plants the year around tended by my aunts, the New England reed organ on which my father could play at least the air and the bass of sundry gospel hymns, of which new volumes were appearing frequently even then. The rag carpet was home made and received annual airings and poundings to rid it of plentiful amounts of dirt. In these two rooms, the family "lived." For sleeping there were two bedrooms downstairs and the parlor bedroom which also served as the borning room.
>
> . . . The pantry adjoined, or was even part of, the summer kitchen. It opened off the west side of the kitchen, had many shelves, on one of which the milk was set in pans for the cream to rise so it could be skimmed off to make butter and cheese, both of which were made at home until the establishment of a creamery made it possible to deliver milk there and get butter and cheese in return.
>
> The lower pasture is now grown up to trees, and trees have taken over other areas of the farm. It was a great life while it lasted. But we had no near neighbors. It was 4 miles to the village, 5 miles to the R.R. station and grist mill and 10 miles to the shopping center of Brattleboro. Our only means of travel was one white horse that found a wagon or a sleigh hard to pull up all those hills. There was some social life for the grownups but very little for me. . . .

The social life of the Bacons did not have a rather wide range about the town in view of the lack of rapid transit and the restrictions due to the cows that had to be fed, milked, etc., and in summer located and driven home besides. As one farmer said, "It isn't how many cows do I own, but how many own me."

The Bacons, like many other families in mid to late nineteenth century Putney, soon gave up their farm. The toil and social isolation that Justin Bacon described prompted his family to move, first to Bellows Falls and then to parts west. For similar reasons, many other families migrated to western states like Michigan, Iowa, Minnesota, or California. The trickling effects of families leaving and older generations dying left the town's population at half the size it had once been. As the nineteenth century closed, only 969 inhabitants remained.

Julius Washburn stands in his tobacco field on the Westminster Road in the 1880s. Washburn owned the farm from 1840 to 1908, and his descendants from the Goodell family continued the tradition.

3. Becoming Modern: 1900–1929

Looking back through a veil of 100 years of the most rapid advance of technology in world history, life in the early 1900s seems quaint and crude. However, to those who inhabited the town of Putney at that turn of the century, their world was modern. Hard work was a natural way of life. Many felt that every machine that could possibly be invented had already been invented and that life was as easy as it ever would be. Electricity, telephones, automobiles, and indoor plumbing had started to replace the old-fashioned amenities of the nineteenth century and people acquired them slowly, as they could afford to. Those who owned good farming land had put down roots and were tied to the land. Those who sought greater opportunity and more affordable land had gone further north—or west. The town's industries could support just so many laborers. Others found work that matched the seasons. Most relied on hunting skills, preserving food from their gardens, and ingenuity to see them through the long and often harsh winters.

Natural and Social Landscape

The twentieth century in Putney began like the late nineteenth century that had just ended. The pace was slow and distances were great. The life of the town as a whole revolved around the seasons. Early in the spring when the water was high, companies still floated logs down the Connecticut River to markets in Massachusetts. Villagers would go down to the river and watch the logs float by, in a routine that lasted about a week. Men, horses, and supplies traveled with the logs on large rafts. Once in a while there was a break in the log float, but for the most part they formed a continuous stream. Men tended the logs around the clock and the logging companies supplied food for their crews, prepared by the company cooks.

Fertile farm soil could be found along the Connecticut River Valley, the Sacketts Brook, and the lower areas of West Hill. Farms in these areas of town continued to flourish at the beginning of the twentieth century. Rail transport provided the means to export excess production and brought in needed supplies for residents and farmers. East Putney village maintained a thriving farm community with its own railroad station, school, and post office. A 1901 *Brattleboro Reformer* insert entitled "Picturesque Putney" gave the following account of local farms and landscape:

32

Its most prominent natural features are Sacketts brook, with its broad fertile meadow and valuable falls; the broad swell of West Hill, and the Great Meadow of the Connecticut, with its 500 acres of intervale below.

Sacketts brook is a never failing stream, flowing from the west part of Westminster, receiving many tributary streams and emptying into the Connecticut about a mile east of the village.

The "Street" so called, passes from the village in a northerly direction, west of the [Great] Meadow, for a distance of two miles and is lined with comfortable farm residences the whole distance. It is one of the richest and most populous farming neighborhoods in the county.

The old country road, passing westward to Newfane and Townshend, gradually ascends West Hill, from which the traveler obtains far-reaching and delightful vistas of river, meadow, mountain, forest, and farm. The original growth of hardwood trees on the slopes has been largely replaced by a second growth.

Social life in the early twentieth century revolved around family, work, and church. In 1900 Putney supported four congregations, three in churches near the village center and one that met at Pierce's Hall in East Putney. The number of village churches was reduced to one in 1919 when the Methodist and Baptist congregations formed a federation with the Congregationalists and renamed the prominent Congregational Church on Kimball Hill the Putney Federated Church. Community groups sponsored dances in Putney and

Ice skaters enjoyed skating on the Sacketts Brook in the early 1900s, just above the dam.

Dummerston Center every other Friday night. Piano and fiddle players provided the music for round dances and square dances.

The lucky ones had cars to drive in summer, but most still traveled by horse and wagon. In winter everyone used sleighs because the roads weren't plowed for automobile traffic. Early autos were powered by steam and soon after by gasoline. You had to be 16 to get a license and those first cars, such as the Stanley Steamer and Saxon, could go up to 30 miles per hour. Excessive speed compelled voters to pass a speed ordinance during a special Town Meeting held on August 10, 1907. The ordinance required that automobiles travelling within the limits of the Fire District of the Town of Putney be restricted to a speed of 8 miles per hour. "Proper officers" were required to arrest the owner or driver of any automobile exceeding the speed limit and collect a fine of $10 for each offense.

Neighborhood life and family chores took precedence over other matters for the young. David Hannum Sr., who was born in Putney in 1900, painted a vivid picture of his childhood and the farm he grew up on in a 1988 interview with eighth graders at Putney Central. The old Hannum farm stood at 167 Westminster Road.

> We would get up between 4:30–5:00 in the morning, milk the cows, take them out in the pasture. Eat breakfast. Get the farm work done or go to the woods. Get back in time to milk the cows in the evening. I went to bed at 8:00. People took it for granted that if you did a hard days work, you were tired.

A young Herb Wood displayed his "bounty" from hunting on Putney Mountain in the early 1900s.

> For fun we used to have parties and play baseball. We would get together at somebody's house, play games, and have refreshments. Ring-around-the-rosey was popular when I was 6 or 7. They used to show movies in Town Hall and we paid 25¢ to get in. I also used to go fishing. The largest I ever caught was a 23-inch trout down in the Sacketts Brook. Boys used to swim on the Connecticut River and in the Sacketts Brook. Very few girls went swimming in those days.
>
> Christmas wasn't made so much of then. There weren't as many cards and presents. We used to go cut spruce or pine trees and string popcorn around them. We had wax candles, but they were kind of dangerous with the branches. We usually got some new clothes, handmade or store bought. The fancy clothes were store bought. The sweaters were home knit.

It is hard to imagine now, but many 1900s children played openly in the streets and when winter came they rode down the streets on a travois, two sleds hitched together with a wide board across that sat five or six kids. Sledders began at the top of West Hill or Kimball Hill, crossed what is now Main Street, and finished their run down Hi-Lo Biddy Road (recently renamed Mill Street). It took so long to complete the course that kids would only make one or two trips per day, begging uphill rides from passing sleigh traffic. Travois sledding was popular on the East Putney side of town, too. There, sled riders would begin at the Town Farm, cross Route 5 and go over to what was known as Slab Hollow in East Putney where the four corners are located near the former home of Eddie Stockwell.

"Higher education" meant high school education in the early 1900s. Off and on, the Central School offered a few grades of high school. More often, students traveled to Brattleboro. Some took the train while many boarded with families in Brattleboro. Dave Hannum Sr. described travel by train and his high school experience:

> By 1914 I started high school in Brattleboro. We walked from my house to the railroad station which was down below where the Putney Inn is now. Then we took the train to Brattleboro. We used to leave the station about 8:30 in the morning and arrive back home at 6:00 at night. Then we walked back home. Some of the children had to walk about 5–6 miles to get to the station.

As the century developed, district schools consolidated to form the current Putney Central School, and the greater Brattleboro area formed a supervisory union to offer high school and vocational training. The history of Putney published by the Fortnightly Club in 1953 describes the early one-room school districts in detail. The Historical Society has even more information on file through records, documents, and photographs.

Business Development

Senator George Aiken, Putney's most famous citizen, came of age in the early 1900s. Born in 1892, Aiken attended the little red schoolhouse known as District 5 and later began fruit and berry orchards on the West Hill. In addition to his own orchard, Aiken planted the first apple trees for Bill Darrow Sr. and his brother George at Green Mountain Orchards. In his young adult life, Aiken was well known in the nursery trade as the first to cultivate, grow, and sell wildflowers and ferns. He built New England's largest raspberry business, before finally entering a career in politics in 1931.

The town's population was in steady decline during Aiken's youth, reaching a low of 760 in 1920. Putney struggled to maintain its economic mix of farming, manufacturing, and small businesses and most families brought in income through a variety of means. Many women worked at part-time jobs outside of the home. A 1901 insert from the *Brattleboro Reformer* couched the economic conditions with a positive spin:

> Trade is not over-done, but is active and well-organized on a scale adequate to the needs of the community. . . . In dairying, the farmer may protect his interests by a three-fold choice, the sale of milk at Boston, the creamery, or private dairying. . . . The manufacturers are in the varied lines of wood and paper. They carry a large payroll and the operatives furnish an excellent market for the surplus products of the farm, the orchard and the garden. . . ."

Businesses came and went, much as they do today. Few establishments passed from one generation to the next, with the exception of farms. Many residents worked outside of the home and maintained small farms as well. Others focused on farming or provided the day labor for the few small factories in operation. Dave Hannum Sr. described the farming that took place around the West Hill in his 1988 interview. Leon Wood had a farm up on Putney Mountain and Cliff Cory had a farm where the Green Mountain Orchards would begin in 1914. Other farmers, who leased land on the mountain, used to turn the cows out on the first of May and bring them in at the beginning of November. Farm hands and young children used to have to go up and "salt" them once a week and check to make sure they were okay. The cows wore metal tags with their names in their ears so that they could be identified.

People lumbered on Putney Mountain, too, and brought their logs back with a horse and sled. Lumbering was one of many ventures that kept small farms viable. A day's work got a 500-foot load of logs cut and transported from Putney Mountain to the local mills. Loggers felled trees for lumber and sent the limbs for firewood.

In a 1988 interview with Putney Central students, Hazel Phelps recounted her life growing up on a farm in East Putney during the early nineteenth century:

> In the summer I had to clean the stables. We had to pick up the eggs. The hens would run around wild and we'd have to find where they nested up and get the eggs from them. We used to have to pick the corn in bushel baskets to send it down to the canning factory in Westminster when we were young. Of course the wagons had huge wheels then. We'd pick a bushel of corn and get it up on the hub of the wheel and then the rim of the wheel. One of us would climb up and get it to the box of the wagon. We would husk corn in the fall.

We had household chores, too. I had to do the lamps or the lanterns. Every other night it would be the lamp or the lantern. The lanterns would be used in the barn for milking and the candles in the house. I often wondered why my mother didn't make us do all the dishes. We had a lot of dishes.

The history of the Stowell Manufacturing building illustrates a common tale of businesses that lived only a short while. The property, which served as a tannery until the 1860s, was purchased by George Underwood and Company in 1875 to make toys, chairs, and chamber seats. From there Frank Hall became a temporary owner in 1883 and sold the building to John Stowell in 1885, who then founded Stowell Manufacturing, continuing the production of toys and chairs. In 1916, the Putney Selectmen courted C.E. Bradley Corporation with a lure of tax abatements so that they would move into the then vacant building.

Bradley Corporation planned to manufacture rush back chairs, pen holders, handles, boxes, sleds, vehicles, household articles, chairs, furniture, lumber, wood, fuel, machinery, and any and all articles or commodities in which wood, fabrics, or metals could be a component part. At a special Town Meeting Dr. Bugbee, a temporary owner of the property in 1916, introduced an amendment to extend the tax abatement from five years to ten. Voters approved the tax abatement at the annual Town Meeting of 1916 with the stipulation that manufacturing be continuous for ten years. On December 3, 1918 the building was destroyed by fire, ending the Bradley Corporation's stay in Putney.

George and William Darrow and George Aiken formed a dynamic trio that was "full of beans and ambition." They would go on to influence agriculture and politics for major portions of the twentieth century.

The personal audio-taped recollections of Minnie Wood, who worked at C.E. Bradley Corporation for its brief tenure in Putney, foreshadowed the shift from self-sufficient town to "bedroom community" that would take place gradually throughout the twentieth century: "I worked over at the pencil factory at Bradley's. The pencils were turned out of wood and then the lead put in. The pencils would come to us and then we'd put the tin and rubber onto them with a punch to hold them in place. When the factory closed, I had to go to work in Brattleboro at the cotton mill."

As the century progressed into more modern times, new activities slowly developed through the ingenuity of folks who could turn good ideas into a little bit of income. Glenn Davis, the only child of Simon and Nyra Davis who owned the general store from 1915 to 1949, remembered what it was like for his parents as they tried to earn a living in hard times. Born in 1923 in the upstairs room of the Putney General Store (then known as S.L. Davis), Glenn spent his youth helping tend to the business his parents purchased from A.M. Corser. He explained this challenge as he described some of his father's strategies for coping:

> The SL Davis barn, located in what is now Sandglass Theater, went hand and glove with my father's business and the general store. . . . He created an order route in East Putney and Dummerston and Putney Village. He did this with a horse and wagon. Mondays were the day to go to Dummerston and take

Men are cutting ice on the Connecticut River around the turn of the twentieth century for Fred Austin's ice business.

orders. And when they came back that afternoon, and late into the evening, they would put up the orders. And then on Tuesday, a regular freight type wagon with groceries and whatever they may have ordered, were put into individual crates and away they would go to Dummerston and make their deliveries. [He kept a similar routine for East Putney and Putney village.]

When they would make these deliveries, a great deal of barter went on because there wasn't a lot of cash then. You would be bartering with maple syrup or butter or eggs or maybe potatoes. So, you had this material coming into your store, sometimes in far greater quantities than what you could sell here locally, particularly in dairy butter. Various people were making butter with no particular standards, and it would have all kinds of flavors—strong and so forth. So, what do you do with a product like that? My father had an operation whereby he would send it by railway express, pack it in ice, take it down to the depot and put it on the morning train. It would go into the Boston area and be bought by local government to go into institutions and things.

Many Vermonters bartered with eggs when money was in short supply. In Putney, people would take the eggs to the Hood egg processing plant located on the Island in Bellows Falls. Eggs sold by the crate as unclassified. In the case of S.L. Davis, he would take what the Hood plant offered and then pass the credit on to the customer who had traded him eggs for groceries. Other items of barter included livestock. Watchful merchants would accept bartered items and then wait for prime times to dispose of them. When livestock was accepted, more often than not, the new owner would fatten the animals up and wait for a higher price.

The town kept a public set of scales, located on a triangle area near the current intersection of Main Street and Kimball Hill Road. People used the scales to weigh horses, cows, hay, and so forth. The scales were standardized and made trading easier. Because they were near the general store, the owner usually had the contract to weigh up the items and make a record of them. In S.L. Davis's time, he was paid a quarter for rendering this service. The public scales kept "the doing of business" in full view and as the S.L. Davis example illustrates, there was an incredible integration of farming and other small businesses in the early part of the twentieth century.

Town Government, Public Laws, and Services

While neighborhoods maintained their own amenities in each section of town, the town as a whole provided for certain services including road maintenance and gradually accepted a town-wide responsibility for the costs of schooling. The introduction of funds for permanent highways and a shift from elected to selectboard-appointed road commissioners began in the mid-1910s. It took several years before the town consistently accepted these changes.

Most positions in government were performed on a volunteer basis. The 1915 annual Town Meeting records listed the following paid positions and their associated compensation:

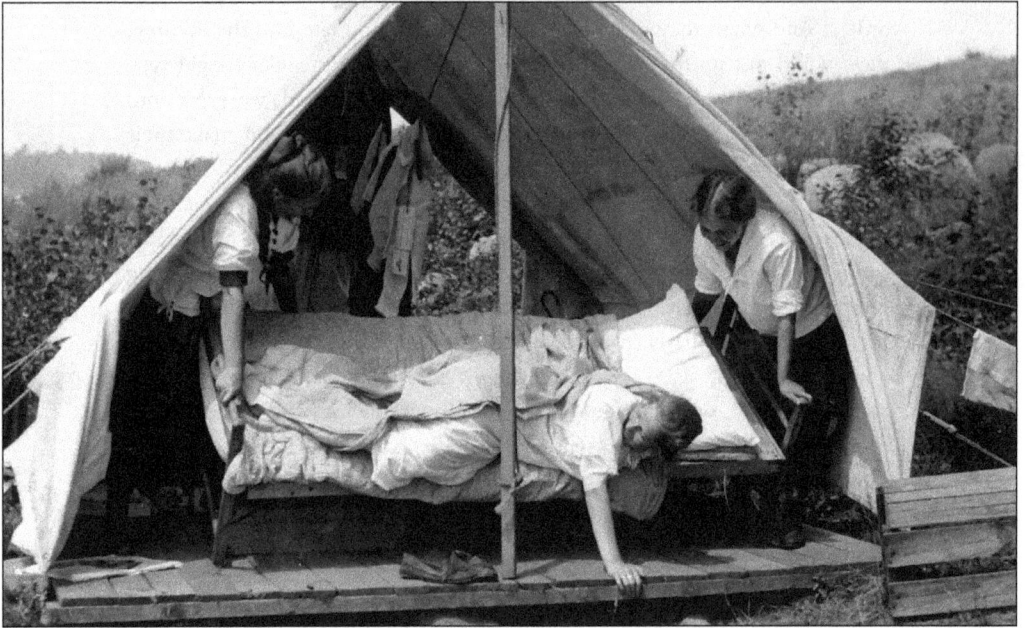

Maria MacMillan Darrow supervised the female workers in the Cuthbert raspberry field planted at Aiken's farm in 1914 and first harvested in 1914. The girls camped on site and picked the berries that were then shipped by train to Boston, Greenfield, and other towns up and down the rail line.

Road Commissioners spent in highways	25¢ per hour for time actually repairing
Selectmen	$90 per year
Overseer of the Poor	$65 per year
Auditors	$2 per day
Town Clerk	$2 per day for attending meetings
Moderator	$2.50 for attending town meeting
Town Treasurer	$10 per year
all other offices	$2 per day

An annual Town Meeting, stipulated in the original town charters, continues to this very day, held on the first Tuesday of March. These meetings, a tradition throughout New England, show democracy in action as voters decide on local issues and appropriate funds for education and town government. Until 1920 when Congress passed the Nineteenth Amendment to the U.S. Constitution, giving women the right to vote, Town Meeting was conducted by men only. Page 15 of the 1918–1947 *Town Record Book* lists the first women in Putney to take the Freeman's Oath, beginning with Sophia E. White and including 91-year-old Dr. Laura M. Plantz and a young Beatrice Aiken.

Early twentieth century meetings included votes to support Memorial Day celebrations sponsored by the Colonel W.H. Greenwood Post Number 90 of the Grand Army of the Republic (GAR). The other community service funded from the town budget in the early 1900s was the Putney Public Library. Established in 1793 and incorporated in 1800 as a shared library of proprietors and subscribers, financial support from the town budget began in 1897 just after a Board of Trustees formed under the organizational name of the Putney Free Public Library. Monies appropriated to the library from 1900 to 1920 ranged from $100–$200, with fluctuations from year to year.

Selected articles from the Town Report of 1905 provide insight into some of the specific concerns of the day:

> Article 3: To see if license should be granted for the sale of intoxicating liquors.
>
> Article 4: To hear the report of the committee appointed by the special Town Meeting for the purpose of making a report whether a new school house shall be built and to act on the same.
>
> Article 5: To hear the report of the committee appointed at the last meeting to investigate a town telephone system and act on the same.

Voters in this 1905 Town Meeting elected Fred Houghton as town moderator and gave the GAR $75 and the library $200. The issue of a town phone system was set aside until the following March (the outcome of which was never reported in the town record). On the school construction issue, voters appropriated $5,000 to build a schoolhouse, aside from the cost of property. They also voted to hold a special Town Meeting at the "expiration of 60 days" to bond the town for funds to build. The voters decided in the following year to sell the schoolhouse and property of District 2 and to remove the schoolhouse of District 1, but to retain ownership of the property.

The debate regarding intoxicating liquors requires some explanation for modern readers to understand the context of this issue. As already noted in the Crawford-Andrews correspondence of June 1842, members of the temperance movement actively tried to stop the sale and use of alcohol. While the Women's Christian Temperance Union (1874) and the Anti-Saloon League (1893) led a national charge, Vermont had begun its anti-alcohol charge almost 50 years earlier. Through continuous efforts, the Vermont Temperance Society pressured the Vermont State Legislature to pass a bill requiring an annual statewide referendum on alcohol on Town Meeting Day, beginning in March 1847. The referendum went up and down for a few years until it was discontinued and the legislature passed a permanent "no licenses" rule in November 1850. By 1853 the legislature strengthened the anti-alcohol laws with additional "no manufacturing" and "no trafficking" rules that remained in place for 50 years.

In 1903 the rules were softened so that each town was allowed to hold a referendum each year at Town Meeting and the fate of alcohol licenses was decided locally. Putney voted in favor of liquor licenses in 1903, casting 131 yes votes to 97 no. In 1904 the vote narrowed, with 115 yes and 101 no. By 1905 the margin was slim with 107 yes and 106 no. Finally in 1906, liquor licenses were voted down. With the exception of 1910, liquor licenses remained banned in Putney until after Prohibition.

Congress passed the Eighteenth Amendment (Prohibition), which was quickly ratified in 1919. Although laws existed to prohibit sales, use, and manufacturing, Congress entrusted (and funded) the Internal Revenue Service to enforce the laws concerning transportation of alcohol. Because of their proximity to Canada and an extensive network of back roads, practically every Vermont town has stories or tall tales about "souped up" cars that could outrun the revenuers. Bob Goodell told Putney's version:

> Alcohol was called hooch or kerosene 'cause it tasted so bad. The bootleggers would always give you a taste of their best, but what you bought wasn't so good. Where Basketville is now used to be a garage. The fellow who owned the garage was a main link from Canada to New York City. Whenever drivers suspected the feds were on their tail, Parker would open the door to his garage and let the rum runners fly through, come out the other side, and down the steep bank. From there, they would hide until the authorities disappeared.

On the eve of the Great Depression, Putney was still an essentially agricultural small town with few strong ties to the larger economy. Some artifacts of that economy, like telephones, radios, cars, and bootleg liquor, had reached Putney. But the townspeople still looked mainly to themselves and their neighbors for their livelihoods, education, and recreation. It would take the upheavals of Depression and another World War to link the town more closely with the rest of the country.

Warren Willard sits at the door of his blacksmith shop in the early 1900s, located just east of Putney Paper on Mill Street. He owned the shop for 50 years, beginning in 1853.

4. DOING MORE WITH LESS: 1930s

It is often said that Putney was already so poor that no one really noticed the Depression. But the Stock Market crash of 1929 and its aftermath hit Putney hard. The paper mills shut down, the town carried debt and tried to cope in any way it could, teachers' salaries were sharply reduced, and public health became a concern. Some projects sponsored by the federal Works Progress Administration (WPA) helped bring a sense of security while others, although well-intentioned, contributed further to the town's debt load. Onto this scene, at a highly improbable time for new endeavors, entered two fledgling organizations—The Putney School and the Experiment in International Living. Their efforts would contribute substantially to the town's economic well-being and connection with the rest of the world.

GOVERNANCE AND THE LOCAL ECONOMY

The 1930s were years of consistency in Putney's town leadership and always seemed to include at least one farmer on the Board of Selectmen. The School Board remained constant throughout most of the thirties—until George D. Aiken broke the cycle by becoming governor of the State of Vermont in 1937. Amazingly, throughout his tenure as town representative from 1930 through 1934 (serving as speaker of the house for the last two of those years) and as lieutenant governor in 1935 and 1936, Aiken had managed to remain on the School Board. When he resigned from his hometown seat for the term ending in 1939, Aiken was replaced in Putney by Mary Howard. Mrs. Alton C. Adams and Mrs. Henry Frost held the other two seats throughout the decade and into the next. (The School Board was one of three town offices often occupied by women in the 1930s, the other two being library trustees and auditors.)

By 1935 Putney was ready to support a town-wide fire district instead of the previous smaller Village Fire District. The Town Report listed Chief Dwight Smith with J.J. Knight, first assistant chief; and Ernest Parker, second assistant chief. Other named firefighters were David B. Hannum Sr., Leonard Howard, and Elmer Gassett. Major fires noted in town records were the Kathan and Fuller fires (1929), H.F. Jones, a forest fire at Stockwells (1931), George Aplin and D.D. Cory (1932), the Loomis place and George

The town did not budget for transportation expenses to Brattleboro High School. This group from the early 1930s was transported in Dr. Bugbee's Model T.

Gassett (1933), Aiken (1935), the barn at The Putney School (1936), the Vassar Paper Mill (1937), the chemistry room at The Putney School (1937), E. Holton and Holway (1938), and a forest fire on West Hill (1939). Twenty chimney fires per year was the norm—for the prevention of which the department recommended an occasional burning of powdered sulfur. An occasional car or truck fire was also handled.

By 1930, both the Robertson and the Cole Paper Mills sat idle, adding Putney to the list of many small towns feeling the effects of a decade of national excess. People were out of work, the mills were not paying their taxes, and the town treasury was beginning to suffer. The Selectmen kept things going by borrowing from the Vermont-Peoples National Bank and several private citizens, who not only helped out the town, but enjoyed a safe place to invest their savings, collecting a healthy interest payment (4 percent) in the process. In 1929 there were four notes payable on the books to such citizens. By 1939 there were nine—plus $1,954 of the various cemetery funds that had been borrowed to make up the gap caused by unpaid taxes and debt. Pie charts appeared in the Town Report for 1933 to demonstrate where the money was going and where it should have been coming from. In 1933 the missing wedge—representing unpaid taxes—was 10 percent of the pie; in 1938 it was 15 percent. Interest on borrowing peaked at 8 percent of the total budget in 1933.

Overseer of the Poor was a demanding job. The effects of the Depression can be seen in the dramatic increase in poor cases from a total of 3 in 1928 at a cost of $861, to a high of 16 cases in 1939. Mid-decade it ranged between 11 and 13 cases, some of which were just loans until people got back on their feet. The highest year of expense to the town was 1932, which cost the taxpayers $2,487.

A small portion of this expense each year was for an undetermined number of tramps, or "transients" as they were sometimes called in the late thirties. Tramps passed through on the railroad and jumped off for a night's rest before moving on. Each Vermont town was obligated to temporarily provide for indigent tramps. The yearly amount expended on these travelers varied from $11.40 to $65.41 including $7 to $16 spent on wood for the Tramp House, which was located near the present town recycling area and served in earlier times as a town jail.

Whatever interest was available from the $500 Evelyn Whitney fund was earmarked for support of the poor but not always withdrawn. Sometimes it was necessary for the town to acquire the deed to the property of those who were long-term indigents, recouping expenses from rental income and/or the eventual sale. Each individual expense for each case was itemized in the Town Reports of the time, near the front of the booklet, for all to see. These expenses included: cash (rarely), groceries, supplies, medicine, clothing, board, care, glasses, coal, wood, potatoes, operations, hospital, electric light bills, rent of garden, plowing the garden, rent of "shack," pump repairs, stove and bedding, expenses of commitment to an institution, transportation to the Civilian Conservation Corps camp, and burial expenses ($99.75 in 1930).

Old Age Assistance began in 1936 with amounts totaling $1,715 paid to the first 22 Putney applicants that year. Marion R. Merrifield was the "investigator" who was responsible for verifying need and financial situations of the applicants. Her first payment from the town included $15 for her time during the 20 months preceding, during which she had written 87 letters in the "course of the work." Mileage was reimbursed at the rate of 5¢ per mile. By 1939, monthly payments averaging $18.50 and ranging from $5 to $30 were being paid to 15 persons, and Ms. Merrifield received $3.15 for auto expense from the town's general fund.

Winter roads continued to be an expensive undertaking. In 1938 as many as 44 men, including several farmers, worked on the roads at some point during the year, being paid anywhere between 67¢ to $993.36. Farmers also supplemented their incomes selling gravel or renting their trucks for town use. In 1928 inflation had pushed the rates to $3 per day for labor ($3.50 for the road commissioner), $7 per day for a man and his team. Then they plummeted by nearly 50 percent. By 1937 rates had slowly risen back to $2.70 for labor and $10.80 for trucking. In 1938 all amounts were converted to hourly rates: 43 1/2¢ for the road commissioner, 33 1/2¢ for others, $1.20 per hour for trucking, 66 2/3¢ per hour for "teaming," 90¢ per hour for a truck only. Gravel remained at 10¢ per yard and fill was going for 5¢ per yard. Plowing with a truck brought $4 per hour and with a tractor $5.50.

What to do about the idle paper mills occupied a large portion of the Selectmen's time. When taxes were sufficiently overdue for the properties to be put up for sale by the sheriff in 1932, the Selectmen acquired them for a total of $3,965.32 ($2,966.56 for the Cole Mill and $998.76 for the Robertson or "Owl" Mill). As money was available, men were hired to make minor repairs on the buildings while a buyer was sought. Finally, in 1936, a contract was signed to sell both properties to Louis Vassar and Sons for $7,500. Only $500 was ever collected. Vassar Paper Mill, which concentrated its operations in the Cole Mill, never reached the profit-making stage before being destroyed by fire in 1937. Fortunately, the building was well insured by the town, which received $4,375 as compensation for the damages. This time the search for a new buyer produced a man named Wojciech Kazmierczak, who for the sake of those who could not spell or pronounce his name, agreed to be called John Smith. In 1938, for $5,000, only the former Cole Mill was sold to Kazmierczak.

Mr. Kazmierczak, who had spent the 20 years since his arrival at Ellis Island from Poland working and learning in the mills of New England, staked all that he had into the burned out mill. Borrowing against his life insurance policy, he enlisted his son-in-law Frank Potash to move to Putney and help restore the mill. By the summer of 1939, they were making paper with one rebuilt machine and a new crew of workers. Napoleon Martin was hired as foreman at 25¢ per hour. Gib and Ernest Turner, Tom Clark, Robert Prentiss, and others were paid 15¢ per hour. Kazmierczak worked from 7 a.m. until 7 p.m. when Frank relieved him and worked until Kazmierczak returned the next morning. Tony Martin was also trained and became an outstanding machine tender. Kazmierczak's daughter Shirley left high school just weeks before graduation to help with the office and the business end of things. Her starting pay was zero.

Recently Shirley recalled that when there was very little money in the checkbook and since the company hadn't established a credit rating, the necessary supplies would come "Cash on Delivery" (COD). Mr. Kazmierczak would go over to Sy Davis at the corner store and ask to borrow the money to pay for these items. Davis was only too glad to lend the money because he knew that Kazmierczak would reimburse him when a customer sent the company a check for paper. Also, the local help who worked in the mill did business with Davis and could put "a little down" on their bills after receiving their paychecks. Davis was a very good friend and neighbor to the mill.

The 1930s were a time of increased intervention at all levels as people tried to aid each other in times of distress, backed by government programs. The extent of government involvement can be seen by the Putney Town Meeting annual reports. Articles on the warning for Town Meeting in 1930 numbered just 13 and climbed to 29 by the end of the decade. Not all help was financed through government, though. An example from the town records shows that, in recognition of the Depression, Cliff Cory donated 34 hours of his labor in 1933 to the town, cutting brush and working on the "highways at the Dipping Hole Cemetery."

The challenges of the decade made the task of the School Board very difficult. Total school expenses for 1939 only increased by $49 in a 10-year period because of a large decrease in teachers' salaries due to the austerity measures set in place to cope with the Great Depression. Miss Florence Follette, primary room teacher at the Central School and Putney's highest salaried teacher of the period, received $926.25 in 1929. The effects of the financial straits of the town are reflected in the fluctuation of her salary as the decade progressed: 1930, $986.25; 1931, $1,000; 1932, $1,025; 1933, $756.50; 1934, $781; 1935, $792; 1936, $770; 1937, $843; 1938, $825; 1939, $850. Rebates ranging from $3 to $6 per week were eventually offered by the state so that the small, rural schools would not lose their good teachers to higher paying areas. Some assistance was also provided by the WPA Clerical Assistance to Superintendents Project, which provided some learning materials for the classrooms.

In 1994 Beverly Stockwell Cooke described the Number 7 school in East Putney as it was in the 1930s:

Transportation between Westmoreland, NH and Putney continued by bridge or ferry from early settlement days until the tragic accident in 1930. This photo shows Mr. Webber driving the Old Putney Ferry.

Number 7 was rated a "Superior School" . . . [a building of] approximately 50 X 50 [feet]. . . . Almost the entire northern side was taken up by large windows to let in the only light, there being no electricity or even oil lamps. . . . Small windows set nearly to the ceiling on the west let in a minimum amount of daylight. On rainy days the teacher would station herself at the north windows and read to the class if she determined that studies should not be attempted in view of the dimness. . . . The floor plan was divided into the actual class room, then space was provided for a small kitchen area with the opposite side of the center front door taken up by space for the storage of fire wood. Chemical toilets were on the westerly side of the building. On especially frigid days the movable desks were pushed near the stove. . . . The "library" consisted of a couple of dictionaries and a few books on Greek mythology. There was no exchange of books with the big school in town. . . . A supply of new text books was an occasion for much joy. It was a student's obligation to keep his/her books in good order and not to make any damage to school supplies. Pencils and crayons were prized possessions. . . . The little kitchen had an oil stove and the older girls might heat up a pot of milk for cocoa. Another favorite was hot milk with canned tomatoes in it. Milk was provided on a weekly basis by the various parents—all of whom had their own source of supply in one or more cows. Tomatoes were from the supply of those canned by the same parents. . . . [Later,] Rowena Loomis (Goodell) was hired to provide more substantial meals such as a favorite, scalloped potatoes. I am not sure who paid Rowena but it was a highlight of our day as her Dodge auto (owned by Henry & Hazel Phelps) rolled into the yard at 11:45. . . . The East Putney Community Club figured in the school social and artistic activities.

47

Pierce's Hall, owned by Mr. & Mrs. Allan Pierce, was the setting for plays and other occasions that warranted a large hall.

DEPRESSION AND THE NEW DEAL

Some of the Town Meeting articles and activities reflected changes at the federal level. Immediately following the election of Franklin Roosevelt as President, Prohibition was lifted in 1933 and the town had to again take the annual alcohol votes seriously. In 1935, the decision about whether to allow the sale of "malt and vinous beverages" and "spiritous liquors" reappeared as separate articles. By 1938, these two items took priority near the beginning of the warning list. The first one always passed; the second would take nearly 30 years to receive town consent.

Under a WPA application in 1934, the town voted to authorize the selectmen to investigate the feasibility of "harnessing water power available for a municipal power plant and water system" (1934), to deduct 20 percent of the weekly pay of laborers on the town road to apply toward taxes (1935, 1936), to accept and adopt sections of an act of the General Assembly of Vermont 1935 session authorizing Putney to "acquire, establish and construct an electric light and power system," to accept the Mary Andrews pasture as a public picnic ground (1936), to approve the establishment of a national park called "Green Mountain Parkway" as of April 1, 1936, whether to permanently close the road between the residence of Mrs. Charles Starr to the residence of the Society of St. Edmund [old Depot Road or Clay Hill](1937), whether to apply to the state highway commissioner for a foot bridge to be added to the cement bridge near the paper mill (1937), whether to elect a board of cemetery commissioners, whether to purchase a wood lot, whether to adopt Daylight Savings Time (a regular article in 1939), and whether to limit the size of advertising structures to 40 square feet (1938).

A project that kept some of Putney's otherwise unemployed workers busy for a few months was the building of the new cement dam to replace the old wooden Cole Mill dam, which had been extremely weakened by the flood of 1936. The town had retained ownership of the dam and water rights when it sold the mill, as it wanted to ensure that the pond would always be available for fire protection. The town also envisioned someday using the water power to establish a power plant to furnish electricity to the village.

Though delayed for several months by the slow procedures of WPA officials, construction finally began on July 19, 1939 with a crew of 14 WPA-approved men and a foreman from Brattleboro. Only three of the initial crew were Putney men. By September 12, it was obvious that the dam could not be completed before winter at the rate things were progressing, so a representative of the Selectmen made a trip to Montpelier and requested more help. They were given another crew of men from Saxtons River, doubling the time being spent on the work to six days per week instead of three. The next blow was the sharp increase in the cost of steel components due to the war in Europe. However, determined to finish the job before winter, the Selectmen made the decision to push on and swallow the extra expense. When the WPA "labor allotment" was exhausted and the dam still wasn't completed, the Selectmen again took matters into their own hands and hired willing local workers who got the job done.

The impact of the 1936 flood on Harry Tarbox's farm on the Great Meadows was severe.

The engineer and designer of the proposed dam had been hired by the Selectmen to be superintendent of construction as it was felt he would be the most knowledgeable and efficient person for the job. Unfortunately, because the time it took to complete the project stretched far beyond the engineer's original estimate, so did the cost of his supervision. His original figure of $180 escalated to $1,110, contributing to the overall increase of the town's share from $4,000 to $6,131. Still, the Selectmen assured the taxpayers that the dam was indeed a "valuable asset" to the town and claimed that they had been advised by "competent engineers" that the cost would have probably exceeded $10,000 had the dam been built by a private contractor.

HAZARDS AND PLEASURES OF RURAL LIFE

In addition to financial struggles, the 1930s also provided human and natural disasters for everyone to deal with. Ferry service from East Putney to Westmoreland ended forever on August 18, 1930 when a routine evening crossing resulted in tragedy. The official cause of the accident was determined to be the uneven distribution of the weight of the two automobiles that were aboard the ferry operated by A.M. Cushing. The position of the cars was adjusted, but it was too late. Two-thirds of the way across the river, water rushed into the shallow vessel, sinking it before those trapped in one of the cars could escape. Ray Austin, his wife Mildred, baby daughter Marion, and passenger William E. Clark were all claimed by the river. Other passengers Harry Pierce of Keene, New Hampshire and Thomas Carpenter of Putney, along with Mr. Cushing, managed to swim to shore. According to one news report, Carpenter stayed on the boat until the water was up to his neck. Ray and Mildred's nine-year-old son Wayne had opted to stay with his grandmother, who had promised him succotash for dinner that day, rather than make the trip with his family.

Having had but a decade to recover from the disastrous flood of 1927, Putney was hit again in 1936. This time the town received an allotment from the WPA for $10,000 to rebuild roads damaged by the flood and had only to pay for material and the use of trucks for transporting it. In 1938 the town was walloped again with a September hurricane that brought more flooding. The WPA paid $2,334 directly to the laborers and the town paid $2,347 for materials and trucking from the general fund.

Land along the river has always been considered prime farmland due to the benefits of the nutrients deposited whenever the river overflows its banks. In exchange for the fertility of the land, people who worked the farms located there had to face the inevitable floods. Hazel Phelps explained the effect on her and her husband as a young farm couple:

> They had to swim the cows out down at the Tarbox Farm, the farm way at the further end of the meadow. My father would row in a boat and the cows would follow him. He got them all across and put those cows up in their pasture. The cows would swim behind the row boat until they got tired. Then they would just roll over on their side and float. My father would call them, "Come boss. Come boss." Evidently they realized they were in jeopardy. They knew enough to know that.
>
> After one flood, parts of the Great Meadow couldn't be farmed for about seven years. The river dug out about an 18 acre hole up in the north end and all the sand and loam came down and we had 20 acres that had nothing but sand anywhere from 6 inches to 3 feet deep of clear sand. So, you couldn't grow anything on it until after they kept working it and working it. Finally, it came back to a certain degree so they could plant corn there.
>
> There was a certain part of the meadow that was tillable, so they got along as best they could. The banks were good to them. Not only here on the meadow, but all the way down through the valley. You couldn't pay on your bills or on your mortgage. The banks were very lenient and helped us to get around it all. Finally we did.

In the mid-1930s a county health council was organized to address the problem of "backward" children in the schools. Doctors, school superintendents, and other citizens identified reasons why a child might not do well in school and began a program of medical and dental inspections to try to remedy the problems. These programs fit into the scientific concerns of the Vermont Eugenics Society, which was trying to identify the characteristics of "good" children and foster their development. The list of ailments the examiners were looking for:

1. Defective eyesight
2. Enlarged tonsils or adenoids. Often followed by deafness.
3. Poor teeth causing insufficient nourishment.
4. Too much outside work.

5. Anemic children.

6. Poorly fed children.

7. Other physical defects.

8. Subnormal mental development.

Superintendent of Schools Ethel A. Eddy implored that "parents cooperate with the schools in establishing Health Goals for the foundation of better health habits of eating, elimination, sleeping, breathing, personal cleanliness, posture, and care of eyes and teeth." The typical farm diet of salt pork, milk gravy, and baked potatoes underscores the state's concerns about nutrition.

In 1934 a dental hygienist examined 153 Putney children, including 27 of preschool age and found only 14 percent to have no problems while 43 percent had very poor teeth and the other 43 percent were rated as "fair." Later that year, eight children lost their tonsils and two were fitted with glasses. Wayne Austin, Hugh Smead, and Frances Walker (Manix) were among the children to experience tonsillectomies performed on Mary Thwing's kitchen table followed by recuperation in cots on her front porch. At least one of Miss Eddy's goals was reached by the daily dose of cod liver oil still being given each student well into the next decade.

To keep up morale when people were emotionally distressed about the economy, the WPA sponsored a dramatic class and funded the production of plays, which were performed at the Town Hall. Inez Harlow was the director and many townspeople became actors. During the 1920s, rent received by the Town Hall for "moving pictures" ($99.50) and other rentals ($94) almost paid for the expenses of the janitor, the lights, and the coal and wood heat for the year. By 1933 rentals bottomed out at $6. 1938 saw an improvement: $10 came in for dances, $12 from the Grange, and $1.84 for movies. Wrestling matches brought in $60 and, along with use by four other groups, boosted income back up to almost $112. Summer theater was also provided by a New York City troupe in the mid-1930s that conducted rehearsals at Elm Lea Farm and performed on the Community Center stage. After two years, however, residents took offense to the unseemly attire of the city actors who dared to wear shorts on Main Street. After a public controversy reported in local newspapers, the company relocated to Keene, New Hampshire where the police chief pledged that his city would welcome the group, no matter what they wore.

While plays provided a creative outlet and movies gave pure entertainment, another pastime that also gained widespread popularity in the 1930s was the game of baseball. It satisfied the human desire to compete and provided an inexpensive outing for the whole family, whether they were players or spectators. Before Cooper's Field was donated to the Community Center, games were played across the road on what has since become a sand pit. By 1935, there was so much interest in the game the Valley League was formed, which included the towns of Williamsville, Wardsboro, Jamaica, South Londonderry, Newfane, Guilford, Westminster, Townshend, Putney, and two Brattleboro teams. Names of Putney players found in miscellaneous news clippings and an official scorebook from May 1934 to August 1935 include: Aiken, Carpenter, Clark, Farrell, Goodell, P. and S. Howard, Irish, King, Lucianni, McGoff, T. Martin, Mayo, Moore, Morris, Mosher, O'Bryan, Pape, Parle,

B., G., and E. Phelps, H. Punt, M. Reed, Rix, Roberts, Ryan, E. Shufelt, Slade, and C. Wade. At least one other player was known to have played in that era though his career with the railroad may have kept him from being able to play in league games. He was catcher Gordon "Chum" Coomes.

THE PUTNEY SCHOOL AND THE EXPERIMENT IN INTERNATIONAL LIVING

Meanwhile, during those tough economic times, two people whose vision had nothing to do with the improvement of the local economy happened to choose Putney's West Hill as an ideal area to locate their respective headquarters, bringing with them lasting changes in the personality of the town. One was Carmelita Hinton, the other was Donald B. Watt.

Carmelita Hinton was a highly educated woman with progressive ideas about how schools should operate and society should function. After college, Hinton worked for Jane Addams at Hull House in Chicago and learned much from the determination of one of America's most famous champions of social well-being. In her Chicago days, Hinton taught nursery school using the experiential learning methods of John Dewey, enhanced by her husband's engineering sensibilities (he invented and patented the jungle gym). While in Chicago Mrs. Hinton also met Edward Yeomans Sr., her eventual contact with the town of Putney. After Chicago, Hinton spent nine years at the Shady Hill School in Cambridge, Massachusetts, teaching the elementary grades.

As her own children grew older, Hinton's thoughts turned to high school–level education. She took a year's leave in 1934 to write a prospectus entitled *A Small Rural Private School*, which she mailed to almost everyone she knew. A response came from

Carmelita Hinton, her family, and students were ski enthusiasts. This March 1937 photo shows the ski tow at the Putney School, one of the first in Vermont.

Edward Yeomans Sr., telling her that he had friends in Putney, Vermont who wanted to sell their Elm Lea Farm for educational purposes. Elm Lea Farm had been built by Richard Andrews in 1907 as a farm and summer retreat. His two daughters lived in a nearby farm on Holland Hill called Glen Maples. The Andrews sisters attended summer performances in Dummerston at nearby Camp Arden, a camp for teenage girls with a passion for the stage. They admired the spirit and practice of the camp and when their father died, they offered the Elm Lea property to the camp directors, Katherine Jewell Everts and Elizabeth Whitney, proposing that they start a fall-winter-spring school modeled on the principles of Camp Arden. The Arden women accepted the challenge, renovated and added to the farm buildings, and ran the school for one year. After a year Miss Everts and Miss Whitney decided to give up management of the school and focus on the camp.

The Putney School: Aborning gives this account of the first meeting between the Camp Arden women and Mrs. Hinton:

> Women of action and marked ability themselves, they recognized Carmelita's ability and drive. They saw the wheels beginning to turn and felt secure in their decision to let her have the plant for three years, making the stipulation that, should the school succeed, Carmelita would buy the place for about $20,000. She was also to incorporate it non for profit, as soon as possible and the Misses Everts and Whitney were to be members of the Board of Directors, thus retaining a kind of authority in the school.

Fortunately for The Putney School, Ed and Mabel Gray, already at Elm Lea because of their connections to Camp Arden, agreed to stay on and run the physical plant. Clyde Hulett, who had been on the farm for five years as a teamster, also agreed to work for the new school.

Carmelita Hinton brought an impressive list of people to Putney. Of those, Donald and Leslie Watt had the largest immediate effect on the town. The Watts had been living in Syracuse, New York when the first Experiment in International Living group traveled abroad. Donald Watt's vision of promoting peace between nations by encouraging travelers to actually live in homes in their host countries for one month had begun to take shape and prove successful. Their friend Carmelita Hinton led an early group of Experimenters to Germany in 1933. The Watts subsequently enrolled their children in her newly-founded Putney School.

Watt had been searching for a place to establish headquarters from which he could work and expand his program. Awed by the beauty of the site that Mrs. Hinton had chosen to locate her school, he set out to see if there were any other properties nearby that might be for sale. The main feature required was that his children be able to walk to school and the only place available was the George Holt farm. The five-member Watt family put on their skis for an afternoon trek and headed out to take a look at Holt's farm. It is easy to imagine their excitement as they visualized how many places on that rolling 150-acre parcel would make an ideal site for them to build their new home. While awaiting construction, the old farm house was fixed up enough to occupy, and the family eagerly made their move to Putney within the year.

The Watt family's new home, christened "Himmel" would be the subject of exaggerated stories about how large parts of the house were imported from Europe, probably because each room was named after a different country. In reality the only foreign parts of the building itself were the doors. The effect on the town of Putney as a whole was slight in those early days of the organization's presence. The occupants merely added to the mystique that was emanating from the vicinity of West Hill and fostered a degree of distrust among the non-academic population who were going about their business and trying to survive the Depression.

The differences between West Hill and the rest of town would become more pronounced as Putney, along with the rest of the country, became aware of what was really happening in some of the countries that The Experiment was attempting to befriend. Carmelita Hinton's innocent trips to Nazi Germany in 1933 and later would be viewed by some in a different light, colored by a growing awareness of the true nature of Nazism. As America approached war, mistrust of the West Hill crowd and their international connections grew. Local misconceptions notwithstanding, The Putney School played an instrumental role in helping to maintain the town during the Depression. During the September flood of 1938, the school built a makeshift sawmill to turn the wind-fallen trees on its property into useful lumber and students took time off from classes to help with road reconstruction along the Connecticut River. Later, Putney students worked as laborers in local farms and orchards, supplying a scarce resource during the war.

Ironically, the ideals held by members of The Putney School produced as much conflict for them as it did for the onlookers from town. Susan Lloyd describes the situation on page 166 of *The Putney School: A Progressive Experiment*:

> Central to the school was a practiced commitment to world citizenship. As the nation's internationalists veered from crusading in vain for peace to making war, Putney's crusaders moved with them, some suffering deeply over the perversion of the German culture that Putney travelers had learned to admire and that had nurtured several refugee teachers and students. Many mourned the wreckage of international friendships that had held such promise in the heady days of Experiment trips and World Youth Congresses. . . . Though the press continued occasionally to criticize Putney's German connections, its faculty managed to ignore this unwanted publicity.

Putney was probably no worse off during the Depression than many other towns and cities across America. Indeed, its size and self-sufficiency were probably an advantage compared to the devastated industrial centers of the country. The town's leaders soldiered on, doing what they could with very limited means, even as newcomers were laying foundations for recovery and future development on the basis of a broadened world outlook.

5. COPING WITH WAR: 1940–1945

The U.S. entry into World War II dramatically accelerated recovery from a decade of depression and created a demand for nearly everything that Putney could produce, except international peace and harmony. The war effort required personal and civic sacrifices. Rising to these challenges united the community as it had never been before. Organizations were formed that worked for the war effort and also helped to provide for community members in need of assistance. The war was a catalyst for change in Putney as it was throughout the country. New ideas were developed and new people came to town and changed it forever. War preparations were combined with entertainment to ease the hardships.

ON THE EVE OF WAR

After the lean and discouraging 1930s, a new decade brought the promise of renewed productivity to the people of Putney, who then numbered just over 900. The national outlook was steadily improving and there was no reason to believe that Putney would not benefit from the recovering economy. West River Basket Co. was supplying needed jobs, the "upper" paper mill was in full swing by the summer of 1939, and Greenview Tissue Mill, then located in part of the renovated mill building, had started converting some of the paper made by the paper mill into final products. The Experiment in International Living had been steadily growing through 1939 when a total of 233 outbound participants signed up for homestays and group travel abroad, and 108 incoming "experimenters" were brought to the United States for similar experiences. Green Mountain Orchards was producing apples and cider, and the Aiken Nurseries and Greenhouse was growing vegetables and flowers and making Christmas greens in the holiday season. Its 1940 mail order catalog featured 24 pages of trees, vines, shrubs, roses, hardy perennials and ferns, fruit trees, and berry plants.

Despite the positive trends, the town treasury was still experiencing serious deficits. Delinquent taxes reached a peak of 18 percent of total taxes due as the decade began, reflecting the struggle many people still had getting back on their feet. Most of the nearly $10,000 of unpaid taxes that had been turned over to the constable were due on the land

Aiken's Nursery Christmas workers pose at Caddie Fuller's house in 1940.

and livestock of the failing small farmers. While larger farms were holding their own, subsistence farming was on the way out. The lure of a regular paycheck and the idea of freedom from the constant battle with unpredictable Vermont weather saw more and more farms for sale—or abandoned—as their owners gave up and left to seek their fortunes in industry.

In 1940, Putney's listers counted the livestock of 84 farmers who owned anywhere from one milk cow to a herd of 65 milking cows, and between 10 and 1,890 hens. Town totals for that year were: 30 oxen, 29 steers and bulls, 74 dairy calves up to one year old, 194 heifers between the age of one and two years old, 640 cows over two years old, and 5,346 hens. Donald G. Aplin and Joseph Palan were the largest poultry farmers with 1,150 and 1,890 birds respectively. Dairy farms with 20 or more cows were the Goodells, the Bosworth Brothers, George Braley, Robert Cassidy, Henry W. Frost, George Garland, Carroll K. Loomis, Henry Phelps, The Putney School, and George Whitney. There were no sheep included in the inventory. Just over half of the farmers listed had enough livestock to be considered commercial to any degree, while 41 merely kept cows or chickens for their personal needs and perhaps to sell a small amount of butter or an occasional dozen eggs for supplemental cash income.

Tourism had started to pick up and in the summer months there was an influx of tourists and summer people, some of whom began to buy land being vacated by the failing farmers. These seasonal residents brought welcome business to the stores and shops and paid taxes on their properties without adding costs to the schools.

The effects of 180 years of civilization in town had begun to cause problems where refuse was concerned. There had never been any rules about the disposal of household or industrial trash, as there had always been a steep bank beside a road or a spot out behind the barn that served the purpose just fine. Decades later these sites would become treasure troves for collectors of antique bottles and other relics of bygone eras, but in the early 1940s, they were becoming a health hazard. Pollution was not a commonly used word and most people never gave thought to the future impact of their dumping as they rid themselves of unneeded junk.

Popular sites began to attract vermin and emit the odors of discarded animal carcasses. In 1940, the Selectmen finally addressed the problem with the statement: "Several places in town have been made unsightly by using them for the public disposal of rubbish." Their solution: "D.D. Cory has a hole on his property, easily reached from the road, which he wishes filled and has offered for a public dump. We suggest that people having rubbish to throw away inquire at his store and use this dump." For unexplained reasons, Cory's dump was discontinued within a year and by the end of 1941, a public town dump was "located on the old McRae place," near the site of the current Town Garage, and "dumping of any kind elsewhere (was) prohibited." It was still quite acceptable to burn trash in the back yard if a permit was obtained first.

EFFECTS OF THE WAR

Town Meeting in 1940 was the last to be run by George D. Aiken as "The Governor," or just "Gov," as he was affectionately called by everyone who knew him. He was elected that year as "moderator pro tem and for the ensuing year by acclamation." On November 5, 345 of Putney's 398 voters helped to send their moderator to Washington. On January 3, 1941, the governor became Senator Aiken.

One of Aiken's last official acts as governor was to issue a proclamation that fulfilled a proclamation by President Roosevelt and the directives of the Selective Training and Service Act of 1940—requiring "all males who have attained the 21st anniversary of the day of their birth, with certain stipulated exceptions, to present themselves at their accustomed voting places for registration." On October 15, 1940 between 7 a.m. and 9 p.m. "The rooms in the lower hall were made available and placards were posted and a large flag displayed on the outside of the hall." Interestingly, of the 111 men who registered that day, just 53 were native Vermonters and only 17 were born in Putney.

On March 4, 1941, voters expressed their concerns about the world around them. Putney acted on Article 16: "The meeting RESOLVED, That the citizens of this Town rededicate themselves and their efforts to the idea of Freedom and Unity that, for 150 years, under Divine Providence, has guided the thought and action of the People of this State of Vermont." Just three and one half months later, the first personal loss of the impending war was felt at home when news was received that the ship carrying Red Cross Nurse Maxine Loomis to England had been torpedoed on June 26, 1941.

The following year, with the nation now at war, Town Meeting began with a prayer by the Reverend Father Dodge, pastor at Our Lady of Mercy Church. Senator George D. Aiken, returning from Washington to serve as moderator once again, opened the meeting with a short speech in which he suggested that Good Friday be designated as a "time of prayer," requesting that all businesses and schools set aside time from noon until 3 p.m.

Daily life had been fairly predictable in Putney as the depression years moved slowly into memory and people went about the business of rebuilding their economic stability—until Pearl Harbor. In a 1994 program sponsored by the Putney Historical Society entitled "Life on the Home Front," the late Beverly Stockwell Cooke, known as "Bev," recalled the events of December 7, 1941. She and her mother Esther Stockwell had been out collecting balsam cones for the wreaths Esther made at home to fill a large order from a company in Philadelphia. When they returned home, "Aunt Hazel [Phelps] came dashing out and said Pearl Harbor had been bombed. The next day at the [Brattleboro] High School, we tuned in the radio to hear President Roosevelt when he declared war on Japan."

Over the course of the war, more than 125 Putney men and women—over four times the number that had gone to fight in World War I—served the nation, leaving the town feeling empty to those who stayed behind. The gaps they left caused many hardships, yet those who remained worked harder, made do with less, and became more united than ever before. For "the boys" to return safely was everyone's wish and prayer.

A Defense Council was formed in 1941 consisting of John F. Maley, chairman; Dr. H.T. Beattie, director; D.H. Smith, auxiliary fire department; Ernest Parker, police; R.B. Howard, American Legion; Mrs. C.F. Thwing, Red Cross; Miss Carol Brown, Woman's Defense Council. Their mission was described in a directive from Governor Wills to the Council as having two main "fields:"

1. Protection against extensive fires and personal injury.
2. Maintenance and betterment of high standards of health and morale.

The first field was to be the responsibility of the fire and air raid wardens, air raid watchers, police, etc. First aid courses were also to be offered to the general public. The second field was for Putney, as a town, to implement by:

1. doing its utmost in the raising and conserving of foods—for itself, and for other places that cannot raise food,
2. preparing itself to care adequately for people who may be evacuated from danger zones,
3. preparing ourselves individually to answer calls for help from other, perhaps distant, places whose danger is more acute than ours.

The Defense Council reported its activities in the Town Reports for 1942 and 1943:

Salvage work was 98% successful in Putney. The collection system was very expertly organized and carried out by Mrs. E. Harlow and Mrs. J. Scott, co-chairmen, and their workers. Those who so liberally gave of their time, trucks and efforts have done a real job and should be gratified with the results of such splendid team work and co-operation. With the coming of spring, the pile will proceed to a fruitful end—Tokyo, Berlin, and other centers of despotism—with Putney's heartiest good wishes.

. . . The Council urges the people of Putney to adopt a more active part in all phases of the work and not to allow ourselves to be over complacent thereby becoming lax and unprepared. Ennui was never a characteristic of Vermonters, and we hope never will be.

The aircraft observers post was ably manned twenty-four hours a day up to early fall, when orders were received that it was no longer necessary. Now the post is manned one day a week or just enough to keep the organization intact. This came about by the strong defense that has been built up on the coastal boarders. Dr. Beattie, who acted as our director and who gave much of his time to perfecting this organization, also taking his turn on the post, resigned upon leaving town and this office has been filled by the appointment of David Hannum, Sr., whose telephone number is 49. We also acknowledge the good work of Russell Howard in keeping the observation post manned.

RATIONS AND RECREATION

Suddenly, life became full of shortage and inconvenience and this time it was not a matter of having enough money to buy certain staples and necessities, it was a matter of not finding them. As rationing was imposed, farmers found themselves able to buy just half the gasoline needed to keep their farm equipment going—until they figured out that if they requested double what they needed, they might receive a sufficient amount.

Marion Wolcott photographed many Vermont farmers for the Farm Service Administration in 1940. Here Robert W. Cassidy drives his team in front of his farm on Route 5.

The increasing numbers of people who had been able to enjoy the pleasure of owning automobiles saw their newly found mobility abruptly curtailed. "Gas rationing burst my bubble of tooling around the countryside," continued Bev in her "Life on the Home Front" presentation, remembering her experience as a 16-year-old with a new driver's license. She was not to experience the freedom she had envisioned, nor were any of her contemporaries. Merely traveling from one town to another at times required that people obtain an official certificate. Dates of departure and return and the purpose of the trip had to be disclosed. In fact, anyone caught joy riding was punished, as evidenced in this 1943 news item printed in the *Brattleboro Daily Reformer*:

PUTNEY DRIVER LOSES GAS RATION

A and B Books Suspended for 2 Weeks for Fun Motoring
One pleasure driver was without A and B gasoline rations for two weeks today following action of the mileage panel of the local rationing board at another hearing Wednesday evening.

"Our family's 1941 Chevrolet survived but the fenders were falling off by the end of the war," explained Bev, "and that was probably the beginning of a large market for

Putney lost Red Cross Nurse Maxine Loomis when the ship carrying her to England was torpedoed on June 26, 1941.

re-capped tires as those were plentiful during the war years." Fuel oil was rationed but many Putney families were not concerned with that as "all we had were wood stoves anyway." Coffee, cigarettes, nylons, shoes, butter, sugar, and meat also presented challenges: "My parents were aghast that my feet were still growing when shoes were so hard to buy."

"We always shopped in Brattleboro on Saturday mornings and were grateful that the manager of the A&P saved out [some] butter, wrapped in brown paper, for people who lived in outlying towns." Bev recalled how, because her mother and aunt looked so much alike, even though a ration coupon was presented, the store manager refused to give the second of the sisters her pound of butter until they started going to collect their butter together. "We raised our own chicken and pigs but we never ate the cows that died. There was a market in Brattleboro that had a reputation for picking up dead animals and selling the meat. We never shopped there."

After graduating high school in 1943, Bev considered herself very lucky to find a job working for Dewitt's Grocery wholesalers. She was allowed to buy one carton of cigarettes and one pound of bacon per week at wholesale and would sell the cigarettes at retail to her aunt and uncle. Part of her job was to count the ration coupons picked up from the stores by the salesman or delivery person and enter them into a machine. "After that [the coupons] were supposed to be destroyed." Bev quickly added, "I never sold any of the coupons . . . I probably was in the forefront of what is now known as recycling."

An important part of life was a break from the routine of work and a chance to socialize and relax on weekends. Round and square dances were held on many Friday nights at the Community Center in the village and East Putney Community Center at Pierce's Hall. Barn dances were also held in the barn at The Putney School and almost every Saturday night at the Odd Fellows Temple in Brattleboro. In Putney, Danny Graham's orchestra, Vosburgh's orchestra, and others provided the music with Elmer Clark or "Teddy" Glabach serving as "prompters" or "callers." Bev recalled:

> For entertainment, we went to dances at Pierce's Hall. One orchestra came up from Bernardston, Massachusetts for $15 per night. Eventually they had to stop coming as they couldn't get the gas to make the trip so we decided to make our own orchestra. Cub Kathan played the sax, "Junie" Kathan played the piano, Addis Robinson played base [*sic*] fiddle . . .

And Bev borrowed her brother Bradley's drums, even though she "didn't know diddly about playing the drums." She recalled one particular Putney School barn dance this makeshift orchestra played, for which they were paid $5. Bev had a nervous twitch in her leg that night that caused her to drum a little too fast. At the end of a series of numbers, caller Ted Glabach leaned over to Cub Kathan and said, "That was a terrible set!" Cub passed this on to Bev by asking, "can't you slow it down a little?" Bev blamed her twitching leg but was quite certain that was the last time they were invited to play at The Putney School.

Deer season kept the men occupied in the late fall as evidenced by this unsigned editorial in the November 23, 1944 issue of the *Putney Center Reporter*:

Dear seasons starts in Vermont on Tuesday, November 21st and the itch has been started for quite a spell now. For 11 months out of the year the average deer hunter is just another citizen going about the daily round of existence, but along about the first of November, a strange thing happens. John Smith suddenly becomes an Old Dan'l Boone and his home becomes a madhouse. He hunts up a villainous looking knife from somewhere and scrapes away at it with an old whetstone until his wife's hair curls without benefit of a permanent. He climbs in and out of the closets, throwing things right and left and muttering, "Where in heck are those heavy socks I bought last year?" He talks night and day about how he missed that spikehorn seven years ago and why he missed at least a 12 pointer, every other year for the past twenty-five.

This goes on for two or three weeks while his work suffers, his wife becomes a nervous wreck, his friends become either for or "agin" him. At last one fine day he buys a new red hat, gets all dressed up in enough wool to qualify as a small flock of sheep, throws his bag in the back of the car, pecks his wife absent-mindedly on the ear and departs for a shack in the woods where he will pick up a cold, sore feet, an upset stomach, a new crop of tall tales and—perhaps—a deer.

When he returns looking like a derelict or grinning like a Cheshire cat, the disease will be on the wane and probably he will retire for the rest of the winter, behind the paper, until trout season rolls around in the spring.

Though life on the home front went on as close to usual as possible, the effect of the war was ever present. From time to time, soldiers would be able to come home on leave and grab a few fleeting moments of the life they had left behind. Bev recalled how she felt about those brief visits: "It was sad to see fellows at the dances who the next week would be gone . . . back in uniform after a couple of months and then gone again. . . . There was a pervasive sentiment of sadness that went right through everything."

Willingly, those who waited at home for the return of their loved ones did whatever they could to help the war effort from afar. Bev recounted:

In Putney, we rolled, or rather folded, bandages at the home of Henry and Lura Frost [River View Farm] . . . we had Black Outs, plane spotting . . . and patrolling River Road. I remember driving up and down River Road with just parking lights on. It was eerie. . . . I don't know what was expected to possibly happen there.

Putney women did indeed fold surgical dressings for the Red Cross at meetings on Monday and Wednesday afternoons (3 hours), and Tuesday evenings (2 hours) from October 12, 1942, through at least December of 1944. One report boasted a total of 48,723 (including 4,840 done in East Putney) in the first 20 months of the effort. East Putney started its own group and in a total of 39 meetings had folded 13,200 dressings. With the help of seasonal residents and visitors, more was accomplished in the summer months.

When the core group of organizers Mrs. Everett (Inez) Harlow, Mrs. Howard (Arlene) LaMorder, Mrs. John (Betty) Scott, and Harriet Emmes first went to Brattleboro to receive instructions as to how the folding was to be done, they "came back determined

The World War II Lookout Tower, located at Russ Howard's property, was used until the end of the war to search for possible German planes coming up the Connecticut River.

whatever else happened, Putney was to fold them perfectly," according to Alma Jansen's article in a 1944 issue of the *Reporter*. "All loose threads, all broken edges were to be carefully picked off because, as was explained to them, a piece of lint getting into a wound might start infection." It took some time for the women to become expert at this job. After the gauze was inspected for loose threads:

> we were given permission to fold. They were then examined for size and square corners and then two of the monitors gave them a final inspection before they were tied and tied so tightly that 25 dressings measured only an inch and a half. This was because cargo space on ships going to the battle areas was limited. Each dressing has at least six folds, some of them eight. By the end of the first afternoon we were so tense that our necks were stiff, our heads ached, our hands were sore, but now, after many afternoons the folding is easy and we relax.

Everyone relied on the newspapers and the radio for information. "We listened to reports of the planes flying over Europe on the 6 o'clock news . . . and Roosevelt kept the country united by his 'fireside chats' . . . We'd listen for the words, 'My fellow Americans.'" Looking back, Bev felt that most of the news was "white washed" but was forever moved by the "very graphic" images in the first pictures of infantry killed in New Guinea printed in a 1943 copy of *Life* magazine. Those photographs brought the awful reality home to Putney. There were to be even more personal jolts of reality to come.

With restrictions on driving and gasoline rationing, snow wasn't the only factor that stopped automobiles from "cruising."

PUTNEY CENTER REPORTER

Beginning in late 1943, The Community Center and its *Putney Center Reporter* provided a most-welcomed contact with home for every person serving in the armed forces whose address they could obtain. The *Reporter* was a bi-weekly, 4-page mimeographed newspaper started by Mary Sherwood, then director and editor, in November. Other editors and key personnel in this venture included Bessie Braley, Sylvia Braley Barton, Laura Britton, Sylvia Derry, Marie Glabach, Clifford Cory, Luther Howard, Mary G. Howard, Herman Latour, Jean Latour, Mr. and Mrs. E.L. Martin, Esther J. Pratt, Pauline Rogers, Laurence Wade, and William White. Equipment to print the paper was furnished by the Aiken Nursery. Ads by local businesses and donations paid expenses and postage to send the *Reporter* "to all Putney service persons, free as a tribute to them from the people of Putney." (Putney service persons included several Westminster West and Dummerston residents.) Articles and poetry were written by children and any adult who cared to submit a piece. Addresses supplied by families or servicemen themselves were printed to encourage everyone to write to those away from home. Many letters from "the boys" filled the pages for the two years until the war—and the *Reporter*—ended.

An excerpt from a typical letter written by Tony Kray reveals the nostalgia felt by one soldier:

> England (Hell's Angels Bomb Group) July 2, 1944: Will try this evening to throw
> off the undue lethargy that has me in its powerful grip, and write a letter to all. It

has been three years now since I left Mrs. Hinton and Putney. I'd gladly give a small fortune to spend a weekend in the garden spot of Vermont and say Hello to those who know me. Have some of Darrow's cider, stop at Chet's Diner for a few of Clara Smith's / "Ma" Stromberg's hamburgers and to Montville's or Bratt's Dairy Bar for a huge malted milk, see all the boys at Charlie Miller's and then for a square dance at the big barn at the school. . . .

The children were also given a chance to express their feelings. This poem was written by fourth grader Marilyn Austin (Loomis) and appeared in the *Reporter* on November 11, 1943:

War makes us feel sad,
Peace makes us feel glad.
In war we destroy,
In peace we build.
In war we hate,
In peace we help.
We are fighting to be free—
Free from want, and hate and fear.
Let us have peace.

During the holidays, packages filled with goodies and greetings were mailed on behalf of everyone back home to lend some cheer to those who would be far away from the comfort of home. Mrs. Alma Jansen submitted the following humorous story to the *Reporter* for the August 21, 1944 issue:

A TRAVELING CAKE

Someone may send you a cake but that does not mean you will eat it. Last November, because the Government advised Christmas presents to those at sea be sent early, the fruit cake started its travels. It went to a New York embarkation address and from there it went somewhere in the Caribbean Sea but when it arrived, the ship had left and the cake was sent to Baltimore where the ship had gone for repairs. The repairs did not take long and this time they were off for South America so the package was readdressed but it came too late again and was sent to New Orleans. After arriving in New Orleans, the young man went to New London for additional training and the cake went back to the New York address and then to Putney. The Surgical dressing group was tempted to eat it but it had a conscience, and the cake was sent on to the young man. But he had gone again. Back to Putney came the cake—it was now April—and we ate it.

In support of the Community Center's effort to keep the town in touch with the servicemen, many businesses bought advertising in each issue of the *Reporter*. Carol Brown offered Irish Tweeds, the Honesty Farm Press offered stationery for $1, and C.L.

Thwing advertised "cornmeal, hominy, stock grains and Lowe Bros. Paints." A sweet tooth could be satisfied with Caddie Fuller's homemade candies: peanut butter, white and chocolate fudge, and several flavors of lollypops, including her "extremely sticky" ginger lollypops. Dwight Smith sold "homemade baskets," gas, and oil. He also offered "coal, wood, welding, repairing and jobbing." Haircuts were supplied by Latour's Barber Shop, which offered evening hours on certain days. Howard's Garage advertised "Exide batteries, Shell gas, oil, anti-freeze, tires and tubes" and "general repairing." His motto: "When in TROUBLE call US."

Local Business

One could get a sandwich, a newspaper, or a bus ticket at the Sandwich Bar that was operated by J.F. Montville. Friday nights meant the steamed clam special at the Putney Diner (located originally in the lower part of what is now Basketville's parking lot, then later on the south end of what in 2003 is Mountain Paul's General Store at 5 Bellows Falls Road). In early 1945, the Putney Diner was run by Mrs. Napoleon Martin and later Anthony Martin. A few years later it would be moved to Brattleboro to become the Railroad Diner.

Mrs. Myrtie Stromberg often played the piano for guests at her restaurant called Home Lunch located in part of the Putney Fruit Company building (132 Main Street). "This led to a little trouble from time to time as there was no dancing allowed [in restaurants]" Mrs.

J.F. Montville's Sandwich Bar, advertised in the Putney Center Reporter *as "where good friends meet," was a hometown place missed by service men and women in World War II.*

Stromberg's daughter Shirley Ellis recalled in 2002. "When Mom played the piano, we had some good times." As a young child, Shirley also remembers her admiration for Fred Howard who would sit at the counter and eat everything on his plate with a knife—even the peas!

Stores in town that advertised in the *Reporter* included Mellen's Store ("High Grade Meats, Groceries, Fruits, Vegetables"), Kimball Hill; S.L. Davis, General Merchandise (8 Kimball Hill); the new Putney Consumer's Cooperative at the former Robertson's Store (14 Kimball Hill); and the Putney Fruit Store (132 Main Street) operated by William Speno, who somehow managed to get sugar for Putney people when it was in short supply. Cory's Market and General Store served the public (in the southern part of Basketville's current parking lot) until March 1943, when the following ad appeared in the *Brattleboro Reformer*:

> Closing Out . . . Stock Up
>
> Not having a business large enough to have a staff of bookkeepers, stenographers, expert accountants, etc. to comply with present rules, regulations, stamps, points and what not, I will sell at 10% DISCOUNT, ALL MERCHANDISE now on hand consisting of a good assortment of GROCERIES, SHOES, OVERALLS, JUMPERS, TOBACCO, CANDY, CIGARS and things usually found in a general store. Stamps for sugar, coffee, shoes, oil and all point rationed items will be required as usual. SALE BEGINS TODAY AND CONTINUES UNTIL SOLD OUT. Telephone 6 ring 2.

Luther Howard's editorial of May 8, 1944, written for the benefit of the servicemen who received the *Reporter*, summarized the town's economic picture of the time:

> Some of these [industries] are considered essential war work, so men have been deferred to carry on the work, along with the older men, girls and women and younger boys.
>
> The Green View Paper Co. still runs the three shifts as usual and are employing the greatest number of people. They have just opened up a new office where the Everleth's Barber Shop used to be [just north of 132 Main Street] . . . An artesian well has been dug and will furnish them water, which they were in need of.
>
> The West River Basket Co. is also very busy and quite a few women are filling in there very well. . . . In addition to [a large number of baskets], the saw mill is doing a rushing business as farmers and lumbermen are bringing in logs every day and these are being cut up into boards.
>
> Aiken Nurseries have begun their spring work as usual, and both men and women are helping here to get it started. Tomato, cabbage and pepper plants are raised from seed in their greenhouse and have a very ready market, for the Victory gardens.
>
> . . . the former Miller garage and the Old Parker garage have been closed on account of the gas rationing and scarcity of help. As there is a great amount of repair work to be done, there is a need for more mechanics.

In the fall of 1944, there was an urgent need for apple pickers. Due to war only a third of the regular crop at Darrow's had been picked with just a week to go before all remaining apples would be "on the ground." The farm labor assistant asked for pledges of labor to "be sent in at once, and those persons who have already signed up should go into the orchards as soon as possible." Special efforts were made by students from The Putney School and Putney Central to pick up "hurricane drops" at the Cooper, Darrow, and Scott orchards.

Putney Paper enjoyed a healthy business, making paper six-and-one-half days per week. Monthly forms disclosing the number of tons of raw material that would be purchased had to be filed with the Office of Price Administration. The fact that prices and wages were frozen was helpful as raw materials were allocated fairly to both small and large paper mills. The mill was allocated bleached sulphite and ground wood pulp, purchased from companies in Canada or Penobscot Pulp and Paper Co. in Maine. Shipments previously coming from Sweden were stopped because of the danger of German U-boats sinking the ships.

The Experiment suffered an adverse effect during the war. Instability in Europe produced a sharp drop in enrollment, reaching an all-time low of just five outbound participants to South America in 1943, with zero incoming for the years 1941, 1942, and 1943. The numbers slowly improved by the end of the decade, but it would be several more years before the organization would become a major employer in Putney again.

COMMUNITY ORGANIZATIONS HELP OUT AND WAIT FOR NEWS

In addition to the Community Center, organizations active in the era included the Masons, Putney Women's Club, the Putney Daughters, the Golden Ace Club, The Grange, The American Legion, The East Putney Community Club, the Women's Association (of the Federated Church), the Woman's Civic Improvement Committee, and one or more dramatic clubs. As the war raged on, new activities were added and enthusiastically attended. War Bond drives were a good excuse to have a party. Publicity was supplied by the *Brattleboro Daily Reformer*:

> Plans for a War Bond party and dance in Putney town hall April 30 [1943], the final day of Windham County's $1,000,000 drive have been completed by Town Chairman Philip Chase and Mrs. Alfred Jansen, chairman of the women's division. The party will start at 8 p.m. County Chairman Henry Z. Persons will be the guest speaker. There also will be a talk by a Putney man. A motion picture will be followed by square dancing.
>
> The dance with Mrs. John [Jack] Caldwell of Putney in charge, is to be called a point ration square dance. Admission to the party and dance will be by purchase of War Savings Stamps on sale at the door.
>
> . . . Transportation will be arranged so that Putney people who care to attend the party may do so.

The party was a success with the "last spectacular sale of a $500 bond" bringing the total for the evening to $1,500, according to the paper. "That, added to those already sold at the post office brought Putney's April contribution to the Second War Loan to $4900."

In less than a week's time after the official Third War Loan drive opened, Putney reached its quota of $7069. The latest report shows the sales total $10,275. This is due to the wonderful response of the townspeople and several organizations. The untiring efforts of volunteers have been a tremendous help in this drive.

Vermont towns like Putney participated in a total of eight Victory Loan Campaigns (or War Loan Campaigns), subscribing collectively more than $300 million in War Savings Bonds. In January 1945, eighth-grader Laurence Wade organized a drive to sell War Savings Stamps at Putney Central School, in honor of those in the service: 268 service men and women were "honored" by the sale of $116.10 in stamps. Putney Paper was presented with a special flag for its 100 percent participation in the U.S. War Bond campaign. Every single employee had either 25¢ or 50¢ per week deducted from their pay towards the purchase of bonds. By the end of 1945, thrifty Vermonters still kept their bonds, maintaining one of the lowest redemption rates in the nation.

Every other month there was a collection of paper, rags, rugs, mattresses, and flattened tin cans. Scrap metal was also collected house-to-house and there was a bin placed near the Town Hall where cans could be dropped off for later transport to a storage depot in Brattleboro. Putney also contributed generously to the National War Fund, raising 121 percent of its $700 quota in 1943, 106 percent of its quota in 1944, and 112 percent of its quota in 1945. In addition to its participation in the national efforts, Putney had its own "War Chest," raising $1,095.15 in 1943—$530.39 of which was from the sale of scrap. $45 was paid out for "Russian relief."

The Community Center served as an important social outlet in the 1940s, producing a newsletter and sponsoring many teen activities such as the game night shown here.

In addition to news of happenings in Putney, the *Reporter* printed every piece of news made available about those in the service—promotions, medals, assignments, discharges, and who was home on leave. The inevitable announcements about those wounded or killed came as a very personal loss to an entire small town. Westminster West's Douglas Bensenhaver, 19, died on December 21, 1944. Putney's Captain John Verret, Chaplain of the 507th Parachute Troops, was killed in action in France in January 1945.

Missing in action was also terrifying news, as was "prisoner of the German government." Fortunately two of those stories in Putney had happy endings. Private Alvah "Mike" Jones was reported missing in action December 21, 1944 following the Battle of the Bulge. Sometime in March of 1945, his mother Mrs. Howard Jones received a card postmarked January 25 from a German prison camp. The first official confirmation from U.S. sources was received in mid-April just prior to the receipt of news that Mike had been liberated by the Allied advance into Germany.

Wayne Austin, an engineer-gunner on a B26 Marauder, was reported missing in action "in the European area" on July 12, 1944. Until his release from prison camp on April 21, 1945, his family received just two cards: one in September 1944 and one in January 1945. By the end of June 1945 he was back in the States, but spent many weeks recuperating in hospitals. It was many years before Wayne was ready to talk freely about his experiences.

In 1999, an article written by Gary Turbak entitled "Death March Across Germany" appeared in the April issue of the VFW magazine and told the story of what happened to Wayne and the other American airmen captured with him. They were forced to march 600 miles in 86 days. Turbak wrote: "It was an odyssey undertaken in the heart of a

Wayne Austin, flight engineer, stood with his crew in this 1942 photo.

terrible German winter fraught with sickness, death and cruelty. Though experienced by thousands of GIs it was all but forgotten by their countrymen."

Inspired by this article, Wayne finally wrote about his own ending of the story:

> When I reached Fallingostel, I knew that I could walk no more and refused to leave when the others walked on. Dr. Caplan put his ear to my chest and told me that I had pneumonia and he couldn't do a thing for me.
>
> I was told that I would be shot, but after three days with no food or water I was liberated by the British. They turned me over to American Control and after I was deloused, showered and (given) clean clothes, I was taken to a large hospital at Rowen, France; I was given blood transfusions and penicillin shots every two hours for two weeks and after many x-rays, they tapped my chest through my back with what felt like huge needles.
>
> After a month I was sent to a hospital in Paris for about five weeks and then on the hospital ship *Arcadia* back to the states. When we were coming into the New York Harbor, I saw the Statue of Liberty and remember saying, "I will never see this side of you again."

An Honor Roll was ceremoniously placed in front of the Town Hall to commemorate World War II veterans and remained there for many years until it began to deteriorate and was placed in the cellar. A search in the year 2000 failed to locate any of its remains.

TOWN AFFAIRS AND CITIZEN CONCERNS

Like most of America, Putney came out of the war years with an inflated economy. Wages had risen considerably, and teachers who started the decade earning between $650 and $850 per year were earning $1,100 to $1,400 per year by 1945, though enrollment in town schools had increased by only four students. Town highway hourly labor rates increased by 79 percent. Greenview Tissue boasted an annual payroll of $40,000 to $50,000 per year. As of February, 1945 West River Basket Company was employing 22 people between its basket shop and sawmill. The booming times would soon see another reversal but, for the moment, everyone was elated that the war was over and life was returning to normal.

By 1945, the town's notes payable had been reduced to $22,000 and liabilities exceeded assets by only $6,599. Delinquent taxes represented less than 2 percent of total taxes. All the while, Putney had taken care of its poor at the cost of an average of 5.3 percent of its total taxes charged. The number of persons or families assisted ranged from six to sixteen between 1939 and 1945 and as many as 29 "tramps" per year were given cash and vouchers for food at a local store.

In 1940, 477 persons were charged with a poll tax that had to be paid in order to vote. In 1941 there were 490. Those away during the war caused the number to drop to as low as 435 in 1944. Delinquent polls declined from 42 percent in 1941 to 19 percent in 1945. By 1946, with returning servicemen, the number of polls for which taxes were assessed jumped to 530. An explanation of the since-abolished poll tax law was printed on the inside cover of Putney's town report for the year ending January 31, 1936:

Sec. 3433. QUALIFICATIONS OF VOTERS. A male or female citizen, twenty-one years of age, who has taken the freeman's oath and whose list, including poll, is taken in a town at the annual assessment preceding a town meeting, and whose poll, old age assistance and flood taxes due such town, were paid prior to FEBRUARY 15 preceding such town meeting, or who has attained the age of twenty-one years subsequent to the last annual assessment, or who is exempt from taxation for any cause, shall, while residing in such town, be a voter in town meeting; but such male citizen or female citizen, if a resident of an incorporated village within such town, shall not vote in town meeting for town road commissioner unless at least 15 per cent of the last highway tax of such incorporated village has been paid to the town treasurer to be expended upon the highways of the town outside of such incorporated village. A person qualified to vote in town meeting under the provisions of this section shall be qualified to vote in all other municipal meetings.

Town Meetings were attended by 25–35 percent of those who qualified to pay poll taxes. During the war years, the sale of beer and wine was always approved, though not by a wide margin. In 1939 it was 89 in favor to 80 against. The sale of "spirituous liquors" would be postponed for many years to come, usually losing by a margin of 2 to 1. Daylight Savings was adopted each year, "provided Brattleboro and Bellows Falls do the same." In 1940 an article to allow the licensing of pinball machines was placed on the warning by petition. The voters of Putney said OK—at $100 per machine. There is no record of anyone buying a license for a pinball machine in that year or the next.

Other action taken during the period: 1940: appropriating $100 for the development of Cooper Athletic field, which had been donated to the Community Center; paying off the U.S. Deposit Fund note in full for the first time in 75 years; and deciding to sell the hearse. 1941: wiring the tramp house for electricity to prevent possible fires from the use of lanterns. 1942: bidding (by Selectmen) to have the Post Office located at the Town Hall; renovating the lower rooms at a cost of $2,136.06, and negotiating a 10-year lease for $500 per year ("the government to pay for heat and lights"). An article requesting "money for enforcing speed laws" was dismissed. 1944: clearing up the title of the Andrews pasture, which the town owned an undivided half interest in, the other half owner "not being clearly known;" raising the salary of the town clerk from $10 to $50 per year (33 voters said yes; 28 said no); setting the pay for firemen "when the siren blows or in case of chimney fires" at $1 for the first hour and 75¢ for "all time spent thereafter."

Town Meeting in 1945 was not moderated by Senator Aiken, who had sent a letter to say he was unable to attend. William H. Darrow Sr. was elected to take his place. Inflation was evident in the decisions made that day with the library receiving $450 rather than the customary $300, the appropriation for "the proper observance of Memorial Day" was increased from $75 to $125 (including $25 for East Putney), and the amount for "permanent highways and resurfacing" being doubled to $400. Selectmen were given the power to regulate parking in the village. A motion was made by Donald Watt of The Experiment in International Living on Article 18 of the warning: "Shall the town vote to prohibit all advertising signs having an area of over 40 square feet over all. This regulation

This early 1940s photo shows Putney Paper.

to go into effect at once. This shall not affect business signs on property which pertain exclusively to the property itself, its sale, its rental or business conducted thereon nor existing direction signs." The motion carried as Putney's first billboard law.

With the war over, concerns including what to do with the observation tower were brought to Town Meeting. The "Freedom Fund" was to take care of its disposal, which must not have been too lengthy a task for it was taken down from its perch and moved across the road to become a shed for a private residence (65 Old Route 5 South). With the gradual build-up of trucks, plows, a "road machine," etc., there became a need for a building large enough to house the town equipment. Those who felt the time was right after the war petitioned for a special Town Meeting in June 1945 to present their plans to the town. The idea was to tear down all the old horse sheds, the hearse and tool houses, and the vault building near and behind the Town Hall to make way for a new town shed. This was to cost no more than $5,000. The back-up plan was to purchase the Bemis garage for about $5,000. The meeting rejected the plan to raze the old sheds by a vote of 96 to 48 and further refused to spend $5,000 to either build or buy a building. Henry Mercure bought the Bemis garage, which Greenview Tissue Mills subsequently bought and occupied until it left Putney for upstate New York.

A preview of the coming age of social services was seen in 1940 when the town first voted to support a public health nurse in cooperation with four other towns at a cost of "3 cents on the dollar of the grand list." At the same time, a Public Health Committee was formed with representatives of "all local organizations" including the school board, town officials, and the Red Cross. Children were examined and immunized against smallpox and diphtheria at the Community Center or the Federated Church before entering school. In the schools, children were also immunized, examined, or given hearing tests as

73

needed. Home visits were made to the sick and to expectant and new mothers. By 1945, use of this service had tripled, the cost had increased by 17 percent, and a "loan closet" had been established at the Putney Telephone office where "sick room supplies" could be borrowed for the asking. The first Public Health nurse was Eleanor Wallace, R.N.; the second, Tirzah Jane Sweet, R.N.

Dr. D.C. DeWolfe, as the town health officer, carried on a one-man crusade to encourage the town to pay more attention to issues involving public health. His annual reports sought to inspire action: "The water and drainage situation is deplorable." "Would also like to bring to your attention the fact there is a penalty attached to the indiscriminate disposal of refuse and dead animals." "Putney's share of the influenza pandemic was a tremendous nuisance to those affected, and of course represented a gross economic loss which was by no means inconsiderable. The matters of sewage disposal, water supplies, and immunization are assuming ever-increasing importance." It would be Town Meeting 1946 before the town was asked if it wanted to hire an engineer to investigate a possible sewer system when the proposed new highway came through. Several property owners in the village had begun to drill artesian wells to solve their water problems but most still struggled with undependable, sometimes contaminated springs, and drank water still carried to their homes through lead pipes.

World War II brought dislocation, hardship, and to some Putney families, real tragedy. But ultimately, the town found itself in better economic condition than it had been at the beginning of the war. A substantial portion of its young males returned to Putney with new skills and a broader view of the world. Putney would never be quite the same.

British refugee students lived in "The English House" during World War II and attended Putney School grades 7–12. The home was originally built by John Humphrey Noyes and later occupied by mill owner John Robertson.

6. Coming of Age: 1945–1959 (or so)

After World War II, Putney, like most of America, entered a period of growth, prosperity, and change. Returning soldiers came home from the war, and later Korea, with new-found skills and interests that would serve them well as they searched for jobs and started new businesses. A space crunch, created by the Baby Boom, required new public schools. Private schools and educational organizations thrived as well. The Putney School attracted highly qualified teachers who were fleeing from war-torn areas in Europe and Asia, and with the war over, the Experiment in International Living expanded its exchange programs. Several new private schools were established at the elementary, undergraduate, and graduate levels. The low price of land attracted out-of-state buyers, while the remaining farmers began to modernize. Town social activities grew as baseball teams expanded and cross-country skiing became internationally recognized. Churches and social clubs supported community events. With the influx of new people and new ideas, the town maintained an interesting political balance in government and at Town Meeting.

Dwight Smith's *Putney News*, published from 1947 until 1958, gives a sense of the 1950s, brightly colored by his personal commentary. Dwight had many strong opinions that he willingly and frequently shared with customers at his garage or distributed through his weekly press.

Growth of Industry

The two major industrial employers in Putney during this period were Basketville and the Putney Paper Mill. Both began as small family-owned businesses and then extended their reach nationally and internationally, both suffered loss through fire and successfully rebuilt, and both provided jobs for townspeople. One is a tale of "local boy makes good" and the other shows how the hard work and dreams of a Polish immigrant came true.

Frank Wilson, founder of Basketville, purchased a sawmill, basket, and bucket shops from Dwight Smith and Ernest Parker in 1941, then called the West River Basket Company. The name originally derived from the West River in Williamsville, the company's original location, and the new owner retained that name until 1961 when it was officially changed to Basketville.

A basket worker weaves at Basketville in the early 1950s.

Wilson had barely assumed ownership when he was drafted into the navy in 1944, forcing him to shut down the shops. After the war he received an early discharge to return home and put his employees back to work. Years later, Frank offered the following description of the business he purchased in his book *Basketville*:

> Picture a pretty junky factory of simple log foundation, cheap wood sideboards, tar-paper siding, up-and-down, irregular flooring, rickety open stairways and everything of the most inexpensive building materials, and you are seeing the basket factory that I purchased. I purchased this for nothing down and one hundred dollars a month, and it included the basic machinery and boiler needed to make splint baskets.

By the end of the 1940s, the West River Basket Company had about 45 workers in its three divisions (baskets, buckets, and sawmill). Many of the workers from this time period made a lifelong career at Basketville. One of the three employees that Frank "inherited" when he purchased the business was Charlie Wade, who spent the remainder of his life as a worker and foreman at the Basket Shop. Other local foremen included William Graham, Ernest Parent, Bill Kissell, Paul Wade, Robert Dunham, and Ronnie Simonds. Frank's brother Holton Wilson was plant manager for 25 years beginning in the late 1950s until he left to concentrate on Basket Barn in Amherst, New Hampshire. Phyllis (Austin) Graham was office manager for many years. Restarting after the war was not easy. In March 1949 an intense fire that took 45 men over two hours to bring under control gutted the Bucket Factory. The fire left 10 men out of work until the factory was reopened.

A glimpse into life in the Basket Shop was given by Robert Dunham to his eighth grade son Charlie in 1988 for a class project at Putney Central School. Robert began working at the shop in the early 1940s when baskets were still made the old way: "by hand with a hammer and nails." Pay was based on the amount of production or "piece work" and so speed meant money:

> One of the biggest things that I had to do [was] learn to spit nails. That means you take nails and put them in your mouth and spit them out, point first. You'd take a handful of new nails, a lot smaller than roofing nails, and spit them out into your fingers, all in the same motion. . . . I used to make these black covers for the baskets. It would take six slats and two cross-slats. There was 24 nails per cover. I used to put out 80 dozen covers per day . . . eight hours, day after day. The only thing I found out was I lost all my teeth from doing that.

Eventually an automatic nailing machine was installed and the practice of nail spitting ended. A contest in the early 1950s was arranged between Robert and the new machine, and the *Brattleboro Reformer* was on hand to cover the event. Robert won. "The people that sold the machine would not believe it," he said. "And even though I beat the machine, that machine was so much easier than putting nails in your mouth!"

In 1956, Wilson purchased the former (Joe) Parker's Garage of bootlegging fame that had been vacated by Greenview Tissue. The new building was partly used for basket manufacturing and storage but it was also to become a lucrative retail outlet—the first of nine subsequent stores along the East Coast, all the way to Venice, Florida. Seeking to compete with other retailers who imported cheaper baskets (made with 25¢ per day labor costs versus 35¢ per hour paid to Putney workers), Wilson also began importing baskets that year. Later, all the parts for making certain "labor-intensive baskets" were prepared from Putney ash and oak wood and shipped to China where they were assembled into baskets to be shipped back to Putney.

Another fire in 1959 destroyed the Basket Shop, which by then was making 1,000 baskets per day. By the end of 1959, a new "fireproof" factory had been built and work was progressing as usual. Many thousands of baskets—especially the picnic baskets equipped with silverware and dishes needed for a picnic, and the popular pie and cake baskets, were shipped by the railroad to companies like Sears & Roebuck, Montgomery Ward, and S&H Green Stamps. Looking back, Wilson admitted, "We never really made much money manufacturing. . . . [The money was] in the retail and importation of merchandise, not from the factories."

Unlike Basketville, Putney Paper had boomed during World War II. Afterwards, however, the demanding market disappeared. Production was reduced to about three days per week and the paper output that couldn't be absorbed by Greenview Tissue was put into inventory. Determined not to let his workers down, Mr. Kazmierczak kept his employees working even though there were no orders. Erving finally took some of the tonnage and things began to ease up a bit.

In his book *Basketville*, Frank Wilson said of Kazmierczak (a.k.a. "John Smith") and Frank Potash, "Few people have worked as hard . . . to start a business." They worked just as hard to rebuild their business following another devastating fire in June of 1946. Kazmierczak kept every last one of the workers on the payroll to rebuild the mill again. It took 10 months, and much of what he had earned for nearly a decade, to be able to start making paper once again.

By then, Earl Stockwell, who had worked for Kazmierczak as a truck driver, had fallen in love and married Kazmierczak 's daughter Shirley. When Earl was discharged from the Air Corps after the war, he was brought into the family business and became a third hand. Earl learned everything there was to know about the mill, working as a fireman, a beaterman, and a machine tender before he assumed a major position in the company. Earl became a good manager because he had walked in the workers' shoes.

Kazmierczak was the chairman of the board of the new corporation, Frank Potash was the president and took charge of the purchasing of raw materials, Shirley became the official secretary and treasurer, and Earl became the vice president and general manager. It remained a family enterprise whose employees were treated with respect and fairness.

Because of a firewall that separated the paper machine and the Greenview Tissue Mill's converting equipment, all of the napkin machines were saved following the fire of 1946. Greenview moved its equipment to what is now the Basketville store. When Putney Paper could no longer furnish them with napkin paper, Greenview decided to move to Pulaski, New York where they bought a paper mill and started their own operation.

After Greenview's move, Kazmierczak decided to have his own converting business. On borrowed money, land was purchased in 1947 just south of the Putney town line in Dummerston and a new building was constructed to house the converting plant. Equipment was purchased from a company in Wisconsin and a sheeter was built from scratch to convert the M.F. tissue (stuffing tissue with a dull finish on both sides). Part of the production from the upper mill was trucked to the Dummerston plant where it was converted into bundles of M.F. tissue, napkins, and toilet tissue.

Yet another fire in 1957 set things back for several more months. Though machines were rebuilt, the demand for M.F. tissue paper had declined considerably. When wood pulp became in short supply and too expensive to buy, the company had to look for less expensive sources. They experimented with all sorts of waste paper materials and became the first paper mill in the country to use so-called "shavings and waste," which was a collection of white envelopes, newspapers, and kraft papers.

Because of the clay and dye in the bales of waste paper, it was necessary to buy special equipment to use with these materials. For several months it was touch-and-go whether the mill could make a product that was acceptable to the trade. After Putney Paper learned the trick of making a number-one M.G. white wrapping tissue, other paper mills started using the same waste materials.

It seemed to those who grew up in Putney in the 1940s and 1950s that everyone in town worked at Putney Paper at one time or another. Because it was "family" owned and operated, it earned the reputation of being the place to go if you needed a job. According to Doug Ellis, "Earl would give everyone a job who asked for it. He would give a person a broom and tell them to start sweeping . . . then [say] 'go to the office when it opens and

A young Earl Stockwell uses the pulper machine at Putney Paper.

tell them who you are.' " For many local men it was a starting job when they were just out of high school. Some, like the Turners who supplied four generations of family members in various positions, stayed on until they retired. In the mid-1950s, many workers began to leave Putney Paper for higher-paying jobs, particularly when the Book Press started up in Brattleboro.

An example of Putney Paper's willingness to give work to those who wanted and needed a job was their employment of Gordon "Gordie" Rhoades. Gordie was somewhat mentally disabled, probably not considered employable by most, but outgoing and friendly. He was given a chance to prove himself a good worker and faithfully did whatever he was instructed to do. If there was nothing else to do at a given moment, he would grab a broom and sweep the floor. If his shift ended and his relief did not show up, he would just keep right on working through the next shift. He was rewarded for his dedication on several occasions by a breakfast home-cooked by Shirley herself—until he began to maneuver this fringe benefit a little too often. Thereafter he was treated to breakfast at the restaurant. Sensitive to occasional unkind treatment by some of his fellow workers, he was staunchly defended by others—especially Kazmierczak when incidents were brought to his attention. Gordie enjoyed employment at the mill for at least 10 years and left due to illness, choosing not to return after his recovery. His new occupation became keeping the town free of discarded bottles, cans, and rubbish. He also enjoyed artistic pursuits that were displayed at the library and presented as gifts to people who gave Gordie rides when he was hitchhiking.

Earl and Shirley Stockwell purchased the business in 1977. The era of the family owned and operated Putney Paper Company/Putney Converting ended on April 14, 1984 when they retired and sold the company to Ashuelot Paper Company of Hinsdale, New Hampshire. They were looking for a company that would keep the mills operating with the same people who had been loyal to them through the "up and down" years. Coincidentally this was the same paper mill where Kazmierczak had been employed from 1917 to 1921.

Growth of Small Businesses

In addition to the two major industries, many small businesses sprang up in the 1950s fueled by the new skills gained through service in the armed forces, creative entrepreneurial endeavors, and the demands of a growing town. Through the initiative of Julie and Bob Rosegrant and many others, the Putney Credit Union received its charter in 1946 and grew by leaps and bounds in its first three years. Share accounts doubled from $3,806 in 1948 to $8,412 in 1949. Loans to enable the growing businesses and property purchases increased from $9,978 in the first year to $22,497 by the second.

The list of new businesses that opened in the late 1940s and 1950s is impressive. The Putney Consumers Cooperative opened its doors in 1941 in the former M.G. Williams store (14 Kimball Hill Road). In 1949, S.L. Davis and his wife Nyra ended their 34-year era at the "corner" store when they sold the business to Oscar and Bessie Cummings. Upon his return from the service, Robert Kathan started Putney Basket Company in the former E.E. Knight wood working shop (on Mill Street). Richard and Eleanor Bradford purchased the former Dwight Smith home (91 Old Route 5) in 1948, complete with stand and gas pumps.

When Tony Kray returned from World War II, he had a thriving radio and television business on the side that took advantage of America's increasing passion for broadcasting. Tony specialized in RCA, Crosley, Zenith, and Emerson brands: "Sales, Service, and Parts." During the fifties he installed a 70-foot tower on which to place his TV antennas. He housed his shop in the old horse sheds behind Our Lady of Mercy Church or at his home at 119 Main Street. The giant tower still stands.

The Vermonter Candy was started in 1950 by Herbert "Stick" Handy in Dorset, Vermont and moved its operation to what is now 22 West Hill Road in 1951. The ell portion of the existing house was converted to a small candy factory and informal retail outlet where the Handy family has made many pounds of peanut, walnut, and cashew brittle for wholesale customers. Not a typical candy store, the retail area is left unlocked during the candy making season (July 4–December 25) and customers come in, weigh up, and bag their purchases, leaving their payment in a box—all on the honor system.

In 1953, armed with his degree in ornamental horticulture from the University of Vermont, third generation Putneyite Lawrence "Larry" Bryant and his wife Carol purchased the former Aiken Nursery and renamed the business The Putney Nursery. Within five years, Larry and Carol built a new sales room and greenhouses facing the current Route 5. The enterprise included a brisk nationwide mail order plant business from late winter through the planting season, retail perennials and wild flowers freshly dug for each customer, greenhouse plants, gardening supplies, gifts, and very knowledgeable advice. In the late fall, a lively group of people worked in a building behind the salesroom to produce wreaths, roping, and other fanciful fresh holiday decorations that were shipped all over the United States. When the pile of unusable balsam was burned, the sweet odor drifted all around the village.

Tourist cabins and roadside stands abounded in 1950s Putney, prompted by an increase in travel due in part to aggressive regional marketing and in part to the higher disposable incomes of many American families. In the early fifties there were at least five people who owned from four to ten cabins, making a town-wide total of 43. In addition, there were four "registered tourist homes." The Duchess Motel was run by Herschel Williams and later became Santa's Motor Court (601 Bellows Falls Road), the Roxy Inn was run by Charles Cager (109 Bellows Falls Road), and the Witzacks established the Shady Brook Cabins (792 Bellows Falls Road). James and Carmen Rand ran the Covered Bridge Gift Shop (183 Bellows Falls Road).

Complementary businesses flourished alongside the motels and cabins, also benefiting from the rise in travel to Vermont. Russ Howard had a filling station and "menagerie" or "miniature zoo," just north of what is now 46 Old Route 5. In 1949 he acquired a baby bobcat that joined his two black bears, four raccoons, three woodchucks, two foxes, one

A young Betsy Mellen relaxes outside the store she ran with her mother Jennie for many years, from the 1930s into the 1980s.

Couples from The Putney School faculty take a rest at an East Putney Community Center dance. Marissa and Felix Lederer are seated as the middle couple.

skunk, three monkeys, and one doe deer that was then 17 years old. This zoo remained an attraction for children for miles around well into the 1950s.

In 1956, Jacob R. (Jack) Poppele came to Putney with a background in radio. Having started WOR in New York and directed Voice of America during the Eisenhower era, he hoped to start a station here. Instead, Poppele and the dozen or so other stockholders of Green Mountain Enterprises decided to build Santa's Land. The park was completed and opened for business in 1958. Jack's brother Richard Poppele and his wife became the managers. Like similar theme parks of the time, Santa's Land attracted local families and those en route to other destinations.

Local craftsmen made items for sale and distribution that drew from the tourist trade. The example of Hugh Smead as he survived a dreaded disease to start a crafts business is especially poignant. Smead Woodcraft's story began in the fall of 1953 when Hugh and Laurea Smead were the parents of two young children, with a third on the way. Hugh worked full time at the Basket Shop in Putney and had been digging a well for the family's drinking water by hand. "His resistance was down because he was working too much," explained Laurea. Suddenly Hugh began to experience pain in his legs. An inaccurate diagnosis by a local doctor missed some of the telltale symptoms of a deadly disease.

Hugh's condition became so critical that he wasn't expected to live. Fortunately, he was stabilized enough to be transferred from the Veterans' Hospital in White River to Mary Hitchcock Hospital in Hanover, New Hampshire where he remained for two months. A new diagnosis confirmed the family's worst fears: Hugh had a paralyzing form of polio. Those eight days when he had not received treatment cost him the use of his legs for the rest of his life. He remained hospitalized for nearly a year, undergoing treatment and therapy. Hugh's fellow workers at the Basket Shop took up a generous collection to help with the family's expenses.

When he was finally able to return home, Hugh could no longer do his old job because it required the use of his legs. At his brother Claude's suggestion, Hugh decided to try to expand his hobby of making duck lawn ornaments into a cutting board business, selling to gift shops. Over time, Hugh not only became self-sufficient, but was able to keep three full-time people busy until he retired and turned the business over to his sons.

EXPANSION OF EDUCATIONAL SERVICES

Public school enrollment soared after the soldiers came home and the Baby Boom began. Developments in the 1950s established a firm place for education as one of the town's major businesses. The Experiment in International Living and The Putney School were joined by the Putney Graduate School, the Cooperative Nursery School and Kindergarten, and Windham College as vibrant educational organizations. For more than ten years, one could go from nursery school through graduate school without leaving Putney, quite a feat for such a small town. Related organizations like Putney Student Travel grew from the fertile environment provided by these educational institutions. By the end of the decade, a new public K-8 school was built and the town of Putney entered into a formal agreement with the Brattleboro Union School District to provide high school services, even while continuing the practice of tuitioning students to schools of their choice.

The Experiment in International Living experienced a recovery in activity in the late 1940s and by the early 1950s employed about 20 people at its main office in Putney. It was annually sending 400 students abroad and receiving about 100 students from other countries assisted by the efforts of offices it had established in 20 different nations. By the mid-1960s, those numbers would grow to 2,000 and 1,000 respectively. Donald B. Watt was still secretary general of the Experiment's annual international meeting, Gordon Boyce had been chosen to serve as the new president, Russell W. Ellis as treasurer, and in 1956, John A. Wallace was appointed executive vice president. All but Gordon Boyce were Putney residents.

Beginning in 1954, both Outbound and Incoming programs experienced substantial increases in participant applications. Donald and Leslie Watt gave up their large chalet-type home to the organization as more office space was needed for the increased staff necessary to process the burgeoning enrollment. When even this proved inadequate for the continuing growth, a conventional office building was constructed in 1958 at a cost of $48,000. A Stran-steel building followed, providing an assembly hall large enough to accommodate a gathering of the entire staff of over 50 people. Gradually, 90 acres of the original 150 acres purchased by the Watts in 1937 was given to the Experiment. A flat cornfield behind the original office (41 Watt Pond Road) eventually became a landing strip for Dr. Wallace's plane. He flew it many times to meetings in New York City. By 1971, the Experiment finally outgrew its Putney campus altogether and moved to its current location on Kipling Road in Brattleboro, now under the umbrella name of World Learning, Inc.

After an intense union battle that nearly tore the school apart, The Putney School was faced with hiring 20 new teachers for the start of the fall session in 1949. Among them were four who would spend the rest of their lives in Putney: Felix and Marisa Lederer, and Steffa and Fernando Gerassi. The Lederers traveled from war-torn Florence, Italy straight to the social freedom of West Hill. The young couple offered many talents to the school. Felix, the son of a German-Jewish conductor who led many significant European orchestras, spoke Italian, French, Latin, and German fluently. Marisa also spoke many languages, had a Ph.D. in history, and had experience as an archivist-librarian.

Fernando Gerassi fought in the Republican army against Franco's forces during the bloody Spanish Civil War. He was also an accomplished painter. Fernando's wife Steffa was born in Czarist Russia to a wealthy, intellectual Ukranian family. Steffa studied in Berlin as an undergraduate and in Paris for her Ph.D. The Gerassis emigrated from Spain to New York City in 1940. By the end of the 1940s, the forces of McCarthyism were keeping a watchful eye on liberal immigrants like the Gerassis, making it impossible for them to find work and in serious danger of persecution. After these experiences, they were eager to leave the urban environment and join The Putney School faculty. In a 1979 interview, Steffa explained her motivation for accepting Carmelita Hinton's offer: "I wanted my husband to have peace in the country. I didn't know that The Putney School is a school that has never peace!"

The Lederers and Gerassis carried the earlier international, intellectual threads of The Putney School into the 1950s and 1960s. Adding to the European perspectives (which were not always in agreement) came the strong voice of Jeffrey Campbell in 1951. Jeff, who prided himself as a man of two races (African and European), brought his training as a pacifist Unitarian minister to the political scene that unfolded in the 1960s. He often referred to himself as "part of the fellowship of the human race" and spent his life preaching and teaching about issues of peace and justice, delivering many orations at Town Meeting.

To supply the school with properly trained future teachers, Carmelita Hinton helped to establish a graduate school for teacher preparation. The Putney Graduate School of Teacher Education was founded in 1949 when the Andrews sisters, who had provided Elm Lea for The Putney School, offered to sell their Glen Maples farm to The Putney School Board of Trustees. Morris Mitchell, a Quaker educator who shared Hinton's values of progressive education and desire for social change, was recruited to become the first director.

For Mitchell, teacher training was simply a means toward the larger end of social change. Anne Fines, an early student at the school, wrote that this emphasis created some tensions and difficulties with students whose goals were different. Mitchell offered this explanation of his educational mission: "We have employed no lecturers, no text books, no quizzes, no examinations, no courses, no grades, no blackboards. Instead we have substituted seminars, careful reading, able resource people, (and) thousands of miles of travel, work, (and) play."

Following an educational philosophy similar to The Putney School and the Experiment in International Living, the Graduate School blended seminar study with field trips, classroom placements, and experiential learning. Though internships at The Putney School were part of the curriculum, social change was foremost. Students traveled to the South to learn about social justice issues first-hand and to offer community service. The Graduate School attracted open and exploring minds. Its students were enthusiastic agents of social change and helped to raise funds to continue the financially ailing school. An example that can still be seen today is the Putney Chair. Designed by student Sam Resnick, the comfortable leather chair sold for $65 and brought needed funds into the school's bank account.

Community attention turned to the public schools soon after World War II. Enrollment at the old Putney Central School, built in 1906 to accommodate 120 students, increased to the point that alternative space had to be found for first graders. The school tax rate set at Town Meeting in 1951 included 50¢ on the grand list "for conversion and maintenance of the Putney Community Center Building for additional classroom space." Article 15, which dealt with a proposal to build a new elementary school on the Community Center's Cooper Field at an estimated cost of $140,000, failed to pass.

In June 1951 a "School Association" was formed and incorporated to look for a suitable site for a new school and to raise money. A town fair, Halloween dance, and Christmas concert, along with donations, raised $1,500 as of March 1952. Plans were to proceed "on an individual basis without calling on the townspeople as taxpayers."

The school directors secured an architect's services for the design of a building in 1953. Article 14 on the warning for the 1953 Meeting proposed a location for the new school. Aldren and Nancy Watson offered 6 acres (near the current 111 River Road) to the town as a gift. After discussion about future changes to Route 5 and other potential plans for a Union Trade High School, the town thanked the Watsons, but declined to accept the gift by a ballot vote of 66 yes to 79 no.

The first school dance was held at Putney Central School in the spring of 1958. The class of 1958 was the first to graduate in the new school, after spending only one month there!

Dwight Smith, who had campaigned to have the town accept the Watson's gift of land, continued to fuel the discussion with comments in his newsletter. On November 14, 1953, he turned up the pressure:

> In visiting the school during Fire Prevention week, the memories of my younger days came in mind—when livestock were loaded into box cars for the Boston Market. Young calves were always loaded last to fill up the corners. The corners in our public schools are full and overflowing. . . . The use of the [Community] Center for the overflow from the center school was only a temporary offer by the Board of Trustees. . . . LET US ALL JOIN HANDS AND HELP GIVE OUR FUTURE VOTERS (THE CHILDREN OF PUTNEY) THE FREEDOM THEY DESERVE AND DISCONTINUE THE OVER CROWDING OF THE BOX CAR.

Despite Smith's passionate plea, discussions about the elementary school were put on hold as the School Board contended with the more pressing issue of high school education. The Town of Putney had been paying to send most of its high school students to Brattleboro High School. Tuition was also paid at varying times to other area schools, including The Putney School and St. Michael's High School. In 1950 the tuition for Brattleboro High School was increased from $150 to $200 per student. To make matters worse, early in the spring of 1954 Putney school directors received notification from Brattleboro High School that, as of fall 1954, it could no longer accept students from Putney. The directors met with those of Brattleboro and several other towns to study the question of what to do. A special committee of five appointed representatives issued its

John Houghton and the boys 4-H club pose for the camera in January of 1950.

report in October 1954. Its recommendation was that Brattleboro and the neighboring towns form a "Union Junior-Senior High School District."

The new Brattleboro Union High School commenced operation in the fall of 1957 and the amount per student paid to the new Union District jumped to $520, a fee almost twice the amount of local tuition to The Putney School. (Tuition had been raised from $275 to $290 in 1956.) Malcolm Jones was elected to serve as the first director from Putney on the new union high school board of directors, with Philip Chase as alternate director. That same year it was decided that the Town School District would pay up to $325 in tuition for students attending private and parochial secondary schools. So, although a union school member, the town continued to support private school tuition stipends until a vote at the 1979 Town Meeting stopped the practice.

Once the high school issue was resolved, attention turned back to Putney's elementary school. Finally, at a Special Meeting held on January 3, 1957, the voters approved the purchase of 150 acres of land bordering Westminster West Road from the estate of Dr. D.C. DeWolfe for $7,500. Along with the land purchase, voters passed a plan to build a new six-classroom building for $165,000. To address the question of some of the old district school properties, the board received voter authorization to rent the Washburn School to artist Fernando Gerassi, to continue renting the West Hill (Red) Schoolhouse to the community nursery school, and to dispose of the old Central School property. While the small district schools fell under the authority of the town through the 1950s, settlement of a legal dispute eventually transferred the buildings to the original property owners and the town no longer had authority over the buildings.

The architects Alfred Granger Associates and N.J. Ojala were engaged and construction began in the spring of 1957. During spring vacation of 1958, desks, books, and supplies were moved into the new building. By the October dedication, enrollment had leapt to 174 students, increasing 23 percent in just one year. The new building was already approaching its space limits!

AGRICULTURAL DEVELOPMENT

Farming as a whole was still fairly healthy in the early 1950s. There were about 80 farms: 40 full-time working farms and 40 diversified farms that had begun to receive income from off-farm activities. There were 15 working dairy farms (defined as those who "had milk jugs out beside the road that Clarence Reed left on returning from Maple Farms Dairy in Brattleboro") with about 375 cows among them. There were eight apple orchards producing commercially and eight flocks of sheep ranging in size from three head to 150. Poultry farms also numbered eight and hatched eggs to raise meat birds. At least 20 farmers made maple sugar in the spring as it provided cash to buy seed, feed, and fertilizer. Some also made maple candies and sold their products beside the road or by mail order. The Maple Croft Shop sold lots of syrup to tourists as did the Cassidys and Frank Harlow.

In preparation for the Putney bicentennial in 1953, Charles Burns summarized farming in Putney by stating that "the small one man farm is very much a thing of the past and farming is done in a specialized way on more acreage to each farm and with modern

Aldren Watson serves candied apples to the East Putney Community Center costume prize winners at Halloween 1950.

farming equipment." Dairy farms large enough to be mentioned by the writer were the Henry Frost Farm (in 2003 the Nopper's River View Farm) and the Hubbard Farm (on the north end of the Great Meadows) with 36 milking cows and a total herd of 64. Mr Frost had suffered a serious fire to his buildings and cattle in 1950. Joseph Palan's "Chicken Farm" was said to have 30,000 pullets being raised for layers and had generated an income of close to $100,000 in 1951. The George Heller Farm "with Dusty Ridge and Garfield farms combined, specialized in beef and sheep, with some chickens." Only two commercial apple orchards were mentioned: The Cooper orchard that employed two "regular" employees and produced 10,000 to 15,000 bushels per year, and the Green Mountain Orchards that produced 30,000 to 40,000 bushels per year and employed six "regular" employees.

Ellwyn Miller farmed on the Great Meadows from 1951 until 1969 and described the changes he witnessed over a lifetime of farming to Putney Central eighth grade students in 1988. Miller's example supports Burns's comments about the modern farm:

> When I started farming, we had a modern farm. We even had a tractor, and there were very few tractors then. The way we planted corn compared with now—we plowed the field, we harrowed it, smooth harrowed it. Then we put a bolt on, or a roller. We made a marker to make some four rows and the whole field was

put into checkers. Then we took a hand jabber and planted the corn in wherever the rows crossed so we could cultivate both ways to control the weeds and witch grass because we had no chemicals to control it the way they do now. . . . When we cut down the corn with a knife, we'd lay it down in the field. Then we'd take a hay wagon and take it up to the silo and put it into a blower, two or three stalks at a time to fill the silo with silage. And we'd shovel it out to feed the cows. It was all handwork. By the time I left the Meadows I had a four-row planter and we used chemicals to control the weeds and grass. You had silo un-loader and you'd push a button and the silage came down. You'd push another button and it fed the cows in the cart. Those changes happened in my lifetime. There are a lot more now and there will be a lot more to come. So, if any of you want to be better farmers, you'd better get a good job so that you can invent machines that will save you all this work.

George and Laura Heller's experience with farming illustrates the financial challenges of the time, especially for those entering farming for the first time, and the shift that many eventually made to other ways of earning a living. When they were married in Grafton in 1950, they had no intentions of making Vermont their home. However, the Korean War changed their plans and before the year was over, they had come to Putney to live.

George began raising cattle on their West Hill farm in 1951, with early-1950s style wifely help from Laura, who fed extra workers much of the time and also worked off the farm. They collaborated with Sam and Marge Bunker, who were farming in Dummerston. George knew Sam from their Putney School days and before. The Heller/Bunker beef business was dependent upon importing young cattle from Lancaster County, Pennsylvania by rail and later truck, feeding them for a year, and then shipping the market-ready cattle back to the Lancaster feedlots.

It wasn't long before the cost of transportation and the less fertile fields of the rocky Vermont soil turned the Hellers toward a different farming venture. By 1953 the Heller farm had 2,000 laying hens. It helped that Stan Hollis, their farming partner, had specialized in poultry. At one point, they housed 7,000 laying hens. It wasn't long before egg auction markets like the Springfield Egg Auction closed their doors and poultry businesses shifted south.

For the Hellers, a house fire was the crowning blow to their poultry business. In the course of rebuilding his home, George discovered that he liked construction and apprenticed with Bill Farrell, "One of the nicest and smartest guys I ever met." Learning the building trade from Farrell set Heller on a career path toward building, design, and eventually architecture. Growth in the 1960s would give him plenty to do.

RECREATION AND CELEBRATION

The end of World War II and the relative prosperity of the 1950s brought many occasions to celebrate and socialize. Organized sporting events became increasingly popular, cross country skiing developed as a national sport, and clubs and churches added to the community spirit. People from all sections of town joined in these events. The 200th anniversary of the signing of the town's charter in 1953 provided an opportunity to reacquaint townspeople with Putney's heritage, mixing memories of the past with visions of a positive future.

Prior to the time when every home had a television, the Putney Community Center and the East Putney Community Club remained social hubs of the town. Samples of activities held on a regular basis were A Good Show and Old Fashioned Sing Amateur Show sponsored by the Putney Hose Co., a talent show sponsored by the Putney Daughters, dances every other Friday night, auctions, and opportunity sales. The Boy Scouts, American Legion, Women's Club, and other groups had regular nights at the Center.

In August 1949, the Community Center and the American Legion sponsored a Putney Field Day on the Cooper Field starting with a "Mammoth Parade" to represent the growth of the town over the previous 30 years. The event, which included a horse show organized by Mr. and Mrs. Oril Clark and Norman Dort, received much attention and well-wishing from area businesses. The grand prize for the parade went to Mrs. Addis (Harriet) Robinson and the 15 children she had dressed as characters from Mother Goose rhymes. A "special first prize" of $1 was given to each of the children. Mr. Smith remarked about the "fine spirit" and hard work that was put into the Field Day and raved about its success in his next newsletter. He wrapped up the subject with the remark: "It was interesting to see that the division between East Putney, Putney, West Hill, and the Legion had disappeared."

The Town Hall was the setting for many social functions. There were community Christmas trees and exercises, "The First Annual Minstrel" (with a "cast of 50 people from Putney and surrounding towns"), Fireman's Balls sponsored by the Putney Hose Co. and the Putney Daughters, and musical variety shows. "Yodeling Slim Clarke and his Western Show" was an especially popular attraction.

The arts for the average citizen of Putney consisted of the entertainment described above. Music was generally of the homespun variety, enjoyed all the more because of audience participation. Many public or private social gatherings would eventually dissolve into impromptu jam sessions where everyone was welcome to join in with their particular instrument, whether it be a trombone (Addis Robinson), a piano (Ike Robinson), or just some spoons (Laurence Wade). Anyone whose name was Kathan or Stockwell would likely be asked to play a tune. If it was a yodeling tune it was Henry Roberts. It all sounded much better than those faraway AM radio stations.

The annual Harvest Festival at Putney School was a much-enjoyed event to which the whole town was invited. In October 1949 over 550 people attended and it was reported that over half of the crowd took part in the greased pig chase. Donald Harlow caught that pig more than once by outsmarting it (or the crowd) and was taken aside the second time by Mrs. Hinton, who tactfully suggested that he let someone else catch the pig the following year. Mrs. Linnie Campbell and Miss Mary Papielska received first prizes that year in baked goods and canned goods, respectively.

Mrs. Hinton and her children were all fond of cross-country skiing and nearly the entire student body participated in this winter activity for four afternoons per week. In 1946 the school's team, including young John Caldwell, attended the Vermont state championships. As the team was sufficiently represented in jumping and alpine events, but lacking for someone to participate in the cross-country races, John decided to give it a competitive try:

I didn't have XC skis, but borrowed my sister's little wooden skis, adjusted the bindings, practiced one day and went to the state meet. We did well and qualified for the New England Championships a week later. So I decided I'd better practice and even went out another day. So I skied a total of four days when I was in high school, two days being consumed by races.

John went on to ski more seriously at Dartmouth and, after besting some of the 1950 U.S. Olympic Nordic skiers, he decided to try out for the Olympic team himself. The toss-up between Nordic and alpine was decided by geography (tryouts for alpine were way out west) so:

I sneaked onto the team for 1952 Oslo and that was that. . . . And the truth is that our whole team got beaten up so badly in Norway that I vowed to myself that if I had anything to do with it, we would never send over another team so ill-prepared. . . . I had already coached one year up north in 1951, had to spend two years in the Navy (during which time I got about six months off to train and participate in the Olympics) until 1953 [when I] took the job at Putney.

Before many more years passed, John's skiing and coaching abilities made Nordic skiing and Putney (School) almost synonymous. His book *The New Cross Country Ski Book*, published in 1971, prepared many future cross-country skiers.

In the winter the fire department encouraged people to skate on the pond above the dam in Sacketts Brook, which extended far back into the meadow and provided a large area to skate on. Tales of wild rides down snowy Kimball Hill or Putney Mountain on toboggans and traverses are told, but to curb that pastime, Dwight Smith, as fire chief, advocated the sanding of roads to discourage kids from "coasting" where they could collide with cars.

The Putney Gun Club was started in 1953 by Bill Lyons and Sonny Wood. They held shooting matches to encourage marksmanship and taught safe handling of firearms to younger members.

In 1951 many people worked long and hard to put in the new ball field at the bottom of the bank below Cooper's field. A major fund-raising effort took place, a road was put in to access the site from Sand Hill Road (aka Pine Street), brush was cut, a grader was hired to smooth out the playing field, and many hours of labor were poured into making the field ready for play. The bank behind the diamond made a natural amphitheater for spectators to enjoy the games. The project seemed a wonderful success—until it rained. With every hard rain, more sand washed out from the road and onto the field—so heavily that after one year of use, the new "lower ball field" was abandoned. Raymond Stockwell carried a souvenir of that ballfield for the rest of his life due to the severe injury to his mouth received from a bat thrown by a Westminster player. The road now leads only to the town's artesian well.

Harris Coomes, hometown athletic star of both baseball and basketball fame, returned from his turn in service in 1956 and enrolled in Windham College (see Chapter 7) where he attended classes for two years. He also played basketball on the Windham team and helped them win notoriety when they were invited to play the preliminary game before the World Championship between the Celtics and the St. Louis Hawks at Boston Gardens in 1957. They defeated Chamberlain Junior College by 8 points. Harris scored 22 points in the game and 46 years later considers that day the "highlight of my life." After their victory, the Windham team was invited to sit behind the Celtics coach to watch the championship game.

Much of the 1953 Town Meeting was devoted to plans for Putney's Bicentennial Celebration. Article 16 was moved that the town appropriate 5¢ on the grand list for the 200th anniversary being organized by Norman Dort. At the suggestion of Julie Rosegrant, Reverend Tyler proposed another 5¢ for the building of a Memorial Green on the Town Hall plot and adjoining properties. This beautification measure simplified the roads with the triangle, eliminated the town scales, and demolished the old town vault. To help with traffic, the Putney Daughters placed new signs on town roads.

In preparation for the celebration, the Town Hall was repainted and a "hard surfaced" road was made to help with mud and dust. Dwight Smith had his own ideas for the Green Committee. He felt the area around the Town Hall–Post Office, which he called "Putney Square," should be black-topped and devoted to parking for the convenience of people seeking to do business in town.

> With a 25-foot black top drive in front of the Town Hall you will stop at Putney Post Office, drive up to the steps, leave the kids in the car, mail the articals [sic] you have brought with you, collect your incoming mail and have been able to keep an eye on the kids that are no different than we were at the same age. You will swing around to a convenient parking place in full view of the General Stores. . . .

On Friday, August 7, 1953, Putney began its bicentennial celebration with two separate dances. Herm Reed and his orchestra played at the Town Hall while Dick Perry and his orchestra, with Ted Glabach calling the dances, kept the Community Center swinging all evening. Saturday the 8th there was a large parade, a band concert, lunch at the Federated Church, a program emceed by Senator Aiken, a chicken barbecue, and a historical pageant at the Town Hall. Sunday the 9th, special services commemorating the event were conducted by Reverend Charles Dodge at Our Lady of Mercy Church and by Reverend Edward Tyler at the Federated Church. An "Old Home Day" luncheon and historic tours in the afternoon followed the services. A framed certificate to commemorate the occasion was received from Putney, England and hangs in Town Hall.

POLITICS, GOVERNANCE, AND PLANNING

The foresighted Selectmen of 1945 (one of whom was Putney's first woman Selectman, Alma Jansen) knew that Putney needed a plan to grow in an orderly and prosperous way. A Planning Committee was formed that worked on road problems and started discussions on water and sewer for the village. It was an advisory group only and had no legal authority, but its activities were reported in the Town Reports for 1946 and 1947.

The first members, representing the three segments of town, were Chairman John H. Caldwell Sr., Thomas Carpenter, William H. Darrow Sr., D.C. DeWolfe, Henry W. Frost, George Gassett, George H. Hamilton, W. Bryant Jones, Frank Potash, and Frank G. Wilson. Robert Rosegrant joined the group in 1947 and the focus shifted to education. There were no reports from this group in the Town Reports from 1948 through 1952 but it received some publicity in Dwight Smith's *Putney News* for February 21, 1948:

> Who is the planning board? Is it a secret organization? Do you ever hear anything about their activities during the year? Who are the key men in the governing power of your tax money? Do the Board of Selectmen represent the voice of the people or do they represent the voice of the planning board? Is your vote at Town Meeting becoming a rubber stamp or is it an expression of your own mind? . . . A good Vermont Yankee enjoys competition and a sharp trade. Be on hand and organize to sell the voters your idea if it is not endorsed by the planning board.

By the time his February 28 issue had gone to the mimeograph machine, Dwight had done some investigating and offered the following retraction to his readers:

Ellwyn Miller stands next to his Farmall Tractor on the Great Meadows in 1963.

We have learned a lot about the PLANNING committee in the past few days. Ask any of the members and they will give you a lot of facts and some new ideas. This is not a SECRET organization. Each member gives its time and judgement on town problems without pay.

At Town Meeting, 1953, Philip Chase moved that the town elect "a Planning Committee for the purpose of considering a Town Manager, and to get together with other towns and their problems; such committee to consist of the three Selectmen and six elected from this meeting, making a nine-man committee." It was so voted and the newly elected official committee included M.W. Howe, Malcolm Jones, Reverend Tyler, Edwin Gray, Dwight Smith, and Russell W. Ellis (chairman). The following year Article 20 asked the voters to elect a five-member planning board that would have the "cooperation and any aid necessary" from all town officials and departments. Mr. Chase this time explained that the board would not include the Selectmen or members of the School Board. The new board, consisting of Alma Tanner, Frank Wilson, Russell Ellis, George Heller, and Henry Frost, helped the listers establish a record for each parcel of property within the town, "a project . . . heartily endorsed as a means to promote equitable and accurate appraisals." It also planned road improvements with an "emphasis . . . to developing area in East Putney and in the West Hill section for real estate."

The selectmen were investigating other areas of municipal development as well, some of which took many years to realize. The Selectmen hired a civil engineer in 1946 to draw up a plan for a new sewer system to be installed in the village. They hired an expert to map the town so that a study could be done about potential growth in the next 25 years and the need for a town water system. Unfortunately, federal funds for that purpose had already been used up and the issue of water would have to wait. Even the desperately needed sewer plans progressed excruciatingly slowly. The new highway was completed through the village in 1955 without the sewer system the Selectmen had hoped to install at the same time. Some of the new maples planted to replace those lost on Main Street due to the widening of the road would later be sacrificed when digging for the sewer lines eventually began in 1976.

After a cutting of 30,000 feet of timber on Putney Mountain authorized in 1949 to be milled for bridge plank, railings, and the future town garage, Carmelita Hinton moved at the Town Meeting of 1953 to establish a town forest with the land. This designation would "promote reforestation, water conservation and good forestry practices." In the spring of 1954, Putney School students planted 1,000 trees on the east slopes of Putney Mountain in "some of the bare pastures." Another 1,000 trees were to be planted in 1955 and Mrs. Hinton suggested it would be nice to have more participation by people from the village.

A requested article in 1952 prohibiting any new "outdoor advertising structures, devices or displays" from being erected without written consent of the Selectmen was defeated by a vote of 56 to 41. Not to give up easily, the question was reintroduced under Article 33, as other business. Robert Rosegrant motioned that "no additional outdoor advertising structures, devices or displays larger than 450 square inches shall be erected, re-erected or

94

maintained . . . without written permission by the Board of Selectmen." That motion was also defeated. In 1953 the question surfaced again and this time the town agreed to instruct the Selectmen to prepare an ordinance "to make Local Regulations on Signs. Final action to be taken in 1954." Dwight Smith's motion to table the article was defeated. Malcolm Jones moved the original article and it was carried. The opposition lines in the sign debate were obviously drawn between West Hill and business interests in the town center and along Route 5. Protecting the charm of the rural area was important to those who did not need large signs to attract tourists.

Disagreements were not confined to local politics. Evidence of differing worldviews is found in Dwight Smith's homemade newspapers. As early as May 6, 1948 he printed a notice of a meeting to be held at the Community Center that evening: "Everyone interested in the principles of world Peace are invited to attend and help organize a world Federalist. Any organization working for world Peace through world education without force of arms and destruction is worthy of individual support." On December 28, 1948 he offered this brief editorial:

> Regardless of your politics these items concern you. Why preach destroy Russia before they destroy us. Why not say, "let us educate Russia to our way of thinking before they educate us to their way." At the present time they believe their way is right as strongly as we believe our system of living and let live is the only right system to guide the world. Education, not bombs, is what we need.

Dwight Smith, who wrote more than ten years of Putney News, *also served as fire chief.*

But fear and loathing of communism, heightened by the Cold War, was felt as strongly in Putney as it was across the entire nation. Conflicts over personal values, fear, and hopes of an ideal society emerged as people sought to realize their interpretations of the meaning of "with equality and justice for all." Carmelita Hinton's youngest daughter Joan, shaken by her own involvement as a scientist on the Manhattan Project, began to work vehemently for peace and eventually went to live in China as a rural agricultural specialist.

Susan Lloyd in *The Putney School* quotes a 1947 speech given by Henry Wallace, the Progressive Party presidential candidate on a visit to The Putney School campus: "The bulk of the world looks on America as the center of World reaction. There is ten times as much danger in the administration's suppression of civil liberties [as] in the Communists." Senator Aiken, an avowed anti-McCarthyist and victim of "Commie" name calling by Republican opponents in his Vermont political campaign for Senate, signed onto Senator Margaret Chase Smith's Declaration of Conscience and Statement of Seven Republican Senators on June 1, 1950. The statement ends with this thought:

> It is high time that we stopped thinking politically as Republicans and Democrats about elections and started thinking patriotically as Americans about national security based on individual freedom. It is high time that we all stopped being tools and victims of totalitarian techniques—techniques that, if continued here unchecked, will surely end what we have come to cherish as the American way of life.

Anxiety that the evil of communism would spread to the United States prompted a lengthy resolution that was read and moved by Carlton Lyons at Town Meeting 1955. Although the resolution passed, a split vote shows the underlying disagreements over whether Communism was the nation's worst enemy. It began:

> Whereas, There are several groups of people, both within and without the United States of America which embrace various political ideologies, the effects of which are to enslave human beings; and
> Whereas, We, the people of Putney, being an informed, religious and patriotic people, do unequivocally reject all such political ideologies. . . .

The resolution went on to stress that the people of Putney wanted to go on record as "upholding the Constitution of the United States," wished to keep their present standard of "freedoms, rights, and privileges" for posterity, and favored the same "for all peoples everywhere." It concluded that the town clerk should be "authorized and instructed" to forward copies of the resolution to Senators Aiken and Flanders and to Representative Prouty. The records indicate "a very short discussion." The ballot vote showed that 59 people voted for the resolution and 31 voted against it. The outcome reflects a sizeable conflict in the attitudes of those who felt that the socialist ideas underlying the communist regimes were worth study and consideration, and those frightened and appalled at the prospect of losing their freedoms.

The Hungarian Revolution in 1956 evoked a strong emotional reaction in the United States because it was one of the first battles of the Cold War. The Hungarian people put up a good fight, but were finally overpowered by the Soviet army. A group of young men aged 18 to 29 from a village outside Budapest escaped to Austria. When the Austrian Experiment in International Living representative cabled the Experiment's Putney office about placing the refugees, the community was eager to help. Homestay families in Putney included Jack and Betts Wallace, Bea Aiken, George and Laura Heller, and the Hamiltons. Laura Heller taught the group to speak English. Many of the Hungarians moved to California, but some still remain in contact with their Putney host families.

Looking back at the events of the late 1940s and 1950s, it is easy to imagine how the different viewpoints, beliefs, values, and experiences of people in Putney would clash as the town coped with the upheavals of the 1960s. Still, the fundamental values of community, independence of thought, industriousness, and respect for nature provided a basis for common ground.

Inez Harlow and Norman Dort work on the Fortnightly Club's history of Putney in 1953.

7. Changing our Ways of Life: 1960s–1970s

Putney's growth accelerated in the 1960s and 1970s at a pace recalling the pioneer days of the 1770s and 1780s. The construction of Interstate 91 opened the town to easy access from population centers in New York and southern New England and the town's many academic institutions drew people as well. Changing values of American society, brought into sharp focus by the Vietnam War, were mirrored in Putney as a younger generation of political activists, musicians, artists, and artisans settled here. The traditional cultures in the town remained vibrant, but commercial and agricultural endeavors were forced to adjust to the changing demands of society.

The Influence of Windham College

During the 1950s and into the 1960s, the center of Putney was a sleepy place with several convenience stores, restaurants, a few garages, a paper mill, and not much else. Open fields graced the spots where the Chittenden Bank and the Sawmill Professional Building now stand. For the most part, townspeople knew each other by name. Educational institutions like The Putney School, the Putney Graduate School (soon to become Antioch-Putney), and the Experiment in International Living kept to themselves on campuses located 4 to 5 miles from the town center. The establishment of Windham College broke with this traditional physical separation between town and gown.

The Fortnightly history tells us that Windham College, founded by Dr. Walter F. Hendricks in 1951, was first called the Vermont Institute of Special Studies. Initially its primary aim was to orient foreign students to the requirements for attending American colleges and to help them achieve language skills. It was authorized to give a two-year associate degree. In 1954, the Board of Trustees renamed the institution Windham College.

Memories about the college's early influences on the town are not particularly vivid. Folks remember seeing a few new people around town who "seemed to have a lot of free time," but who mixed in easily with locals at the restaurant or in the stores. They remember that the college purchased a lot of houses and that local kids were allowed to use the weight room in Windham's "Gray House" on Kimball Hill. One teenager at the time thinks fondly back to one particular college student whose family owned a coffee ranch in South America and was quite wealthy. The young man drove a brand-new 1957 Chevy with a dragon painted on the back of it and would give rides to the Putney youngsters. Reason enough to be remembered in an isolated small town where almost no one had a new car!

Although Dr. Hendricks's intention from the outset was to build a real campus, Windham's downtown college lasted from 1954 until 1966. The college began moving to a self-contained location just above the village when its first two dorms opened in 1964, utilizing then-abundant federal funding. For the first year or two meals were still provided in the old dining hall, which meant that dorm students walked into town for their meals and classes. Once completed, the new campus, built from plans provided by Edward Durrell Stone, remained within easy walking distance of the town center.

To most locals, the college students of the mid-1960s looked like "spoiled brats" who took up all the restaurant booths and tended to block traffic by crossing the streets in bunches or hitchhiking. Students shopped in all of the businesses from time to time, but there were some in which they felt more welcomed than in others. From one Windham College student's perspective, the townspeople didn't know them by name and that made it easier to lump all students together into one negative generality. The college itself did not allow freshmen to have cars and that kept them within the confines of town unless they had friends with cars or hitchhiked into Brattleboro.

Currier Hall, located on Old Depot Road, was one of the main buildings on the Windham College town campus.

The lack of basic conveniences in town presented a real problem for students, especially when it came to banking. While the Putney Credit Union existed, it did not offer checking accounts and complained if students put money in and then withdrew some a week later. As a result, students frequented those places that would extend credit. The Cummings Store (Fickett's General Store after 1974) and Sam's Market became major spots for college student shopping. Not only would Oscar Cummings and Sam Howard extend credit; they hired college students to work in their stores and Cummings Store sold wine and beer. Mellen's Store remained more of a favorite for locals.

Windham College significantly enhanced Putney's reputation in the arts as high caliber writers, musicians, visual artists, actors, and directors were hired to teach. Luckily, many of these talented professors, and some of the students they trained, remained as long-term residents and contributed to the arts in our community long after Windham College closed its doors. Musicians George and Jane Soulos and David and Janet Wells were among those people. George and Jane came to Putney in 1965. George recounts his first days by saying, "It was such a small town and we all thought we were such 'big shits.' I remember wearing a name tag to an orientation party that said 'Music — Mr. Soulos.' No one called me Mr. Soulos."

David Wells joined the Windham faculty in 1968 and Janet "thought she had gone to heaven" when she first saw the town. Putney, with its rustic atmosphere and small town friendliness, seemed like the perfect place to realize a long held fantasy—a summer camp

George Soulos demonstrates how to play the recorder to young children in 1973 at the Windham Fine Arts Building dance studio.

for young musicians to receive intensive study. Within a year, they started looking for a house, spotted their current location at 9 a.m. one day and bought it by 10 a.m. Thus, the Yellow Barn was born. One of Janet's memories of those beginning years shows how enthusiasm can carry an idea through to reality:

> Carol Brown, much to our amazement, stuck twenty dollars into David's pocket. We had never thought about raising money. After that, we put out a shoebox. After the concerts we would sit on our bed and count the donations. We were thrilled when once we had thirty-eight dollars.

The Windham College studio art program brought many significant visual artists to the area. When David Rohn was hired to design the program, he knew good studio artists were needed as teachers if the art department was to compete with other institutions. The college could not afford a competitive salary, but David believed he could lure excellent artists with the promise of creative freedom and an open teaching environment. He was successful and both Peter Forakis and Charles Ginnever came to Windham to teach studio art. Art historians Donald Harrington and Jack Gillahan further enriched the department. Because of the changing political landscape and the new excitement and vitality in the art world, students were asked to think about global situations, to meditate, and to read poetry. Leading conceptual artists from New York created artworks on the Windham campus, notably Carl Andre and Douglas Huebler. The department carried its energy into downtown Putney with performance pieces, pageants, parades, art exhibitions in conventional and non-conventional spaces, and heated debates about the Women's Movement.

Joe Greenhoe was hired to build a theater program in 1969. His first shows were performed in Town Hall and other locations on Main Street. Once completed, the Studio Theatre and the Main Theatre in the Windham Fine Arts Building provided excellent venues for small and large scale theatrical and musical events. Paul Nelson joined the Theater Department in 1971 and started a summer theater program, using his connections with New York City professionals. Six professional actors, one or two directors, and costume designers worked with the students to mount professional quality productions. Gradually, they built a wide and devoted audience that included tourists as well as locals. For the American Bicentennial, Joe wrote a play called *The Equivalent Lands* that tells how Dummerston and Putney were settled. In 1976 he produced a fully staged version and hundreds attended, filling the house for every performance.

While Putney was somewhat divided along town/gown lines, there were also points of crossover. Windham students felt well received by the local congregations and attended Saturday mass at Our Lady of Mercy or Sunday worship at the Federated Church. Around 1960, Bishop Robert Joyce of the Burlington Roman Catholic Diocese proposed building a Newman Center on the Our Lady of Mercy rectory property near Windham's campus buildings on Old Depot Road. The purpose of Newman Centers was to serve the students, teachers, staff, and community of the associated college. Newman Hall was subsequently constructed and Our Lady of Mercy pastor Reverend Paul Hebert SSE became the campus chaplain. He was later followed by Reverend Aime Trehan SSE and Reverend Vincent Mahoney SSE. With gymnasium, classrooms, and kitchen facilities,

Newman Hall became a good place to gather for discussions, socializing, and playing basketball. Once the college moved to its River Road campus, the church continued to use the hall for youth group activities, religious education instruction, church suppers, dances, auctions, and so forth until the mid-1980s.

Religion was one of many ways that Windham students participated in the larger Putney community. College kids would go hunting with local families. Some townspeople dated college students and went to Windham parties. As one alumna said, "Being one of the few girls at the school, you didn't lack for local attention." Occasionally students purchased houses for personal use or for rental and many of them found local jobs to help them get through college.

There was also some friction between the townies and the college students. In the 1950s and early 1960s, local boys "souped up" their cars to hold drag races in the streets, trying to beat the college kids' fancy new cars. Local places like the Putney Inn offered live music on Friday and Saturday nights, attracting college students and locals. After an evening of drinking, tensions would mount as locals felt outnumbered in their own establishments by these newcomers to their community.

While the college's influence on town was massive, it did not last long as an institution. Growing debt, declining enrollments, and conflict between the administration and the faculty marred Windham's final years. Valiant efforts were made by the Board of Directors and by faculty and student leaders to devise new academic programs and sounder financing, but by 1976 the college's problems were life threatening. Johnnie Stones, a former student and subsequent popular Dean of Students, agreed to serve as president of a drastically downsized operation, but the decline continued. In the fall of 1978, broke and unable to secure emergency funding, Windham College reluctantly closed its doors, just one year short of its quarter century mark. Its brief existence had brought much that was positive and enriching to Putney and it was greatly missed by faculty, alumni, and townspeople alike.

INTERSTATE TRANSPORTATION OF PEOPLE, GOODS, AND IDEAS

Although George Aiken had long since shifted his political focus to the U.S. Senate in Washington, D.C., he never forgot his hometown ties to Putney. One of the most significant moves he made regarding our town was the designation of Putney's own Exit 4 on Interstate 91. In keeping with his ability to create catchy phrases that would attract attention (he coined the phrase "The Northeast Kingdom"), Aiken proclaimed Putney "The World's Best Known Small Town."

On December 6, 1961, following a luncheon at Windham College, the Putney Junior Police escorted distinguished guests and onlookers from the dining hall on Old Depot Road to the Putney interchange overpass. Selectmen Roscoe Hodgdon and Roy Hallock, with Morris Mitchell of the Putney Graduate School as master of ceremonies, officially cut the ribbon while "two pretty girls from Windham College, Shelagh Pew and Judith Poppele, held the ends." The ceremony opened 12 miles of highway, leading from Exit 3 to a point near Santa's Land and the Westminster line. To quote a *Brattleboro Reformer* article of time, "This new extension, moreover, should lessen the accident rate, despite the likelihood that it will increase the number of arrests for speeding. Under ordinary circumstances, the latter is preferable to the former."

Turnout for the ribbon cutting was one of the largest that had gathered for a road opening to date, according to Lieutenant Governor Ralph Foote, who was on hand to congratulate the crowd. The *Brattleboro Reformer* reported:

> The line of nearly 150 vehicles, including the fire trucks from Putney, Dummerston and Putney School, cars full of students from Windham College, cars and trucks from Putney Nurseries, Putney Paper, Santa's Land and West River Basket Corp. and many others joined in the celebration by making the short tour on the new link of the Interstate Highway.

Traffic began moving northward on the highway even before the motorcade had completed its tour.

Expectations of rapid growth accompanied construction of the Interstate. George Aiken predicted that within three years the Route 5 traffic would be even heavier than it was in 1961 as crowds from New England were drawn to Putney by the new highway. According to the *Reformer*, "Roadside establishments along Route 5 will suffer, to be sure, but if their experience follows that of other like sections they will find that the region's steadily growing travel volume will prevent their locations from growing up to weeds."

The Windham College students have a little fun with the Putney fire department in the late 1960s while posing for this group shot.

The Putney Inn, which opened in the summer of 1964, was one of the first new businesses to take direct advantage of Interstate travel. Located at Exit 4 North, the inn and motel catered to tourists, while the conference room made it a convenient place to conduct business. A relaxation of the town's spirituous liquor ban allowed the establishment of a cocktail lounge and Rathskeller frequented by locals as well as tourists. An early brochure lists room rates that ranged from $10 per night for a single to $20 per night for four in a room. The brochure also boasted of Putney tourist attractions:

> The surrounding countryside abounds in unique shops, institutions and sporting attractions as well as delightful scenery at all seasons of the year. Carol Brown's well-known Irish tweeds, the world's largest basket store and many other shops in the immediate area provide for hours of enjoyable browsing. Country auctions, antique stores, the Putney Historical Society's museum and Steamtown, USA in Bellows Falls add historical dimension to the region.

The second business directly linked to the Interstate was the service station at Exit 4 South. Technically in the town of Dummerston, the station has been managed or owned by Putney families since its inception. Originally it was the site of Russ Howard's new garage when the course of Route 5 was changed in the 1950s, and was later Rod's Shell before his move to Main Street in 1968. Sun Oil Company, wishing to capitalize on the Exit 4 location, purchased this prime site and erected a new service station. The first operator was Robert (Butch) Goodell Jr., who offered car repair services. Recognizing a better potential for that particular location, subsequent owners Mike and Terry Finnell converted the repair stalls into a thriving convenience store now open 24 hours every day.

A few new businesses flourished and small shops opened on Main Street, but the roadside businesses along Route 5 on the northern side of town took an immediate plunge. Aiken's prediction of increased traffic never materialized. The effect of the Interstate devastated everyone whose income relied on impulse buyers, travelers who wanted one last taste of Vermont products before returning home. Don Harlow recalls that the traffic on Route 5 was so slow, "My kids could play marbles in the road." The 1968 billboard law further reduced tourist trade in Putney, prompting local merchants to dub I-91 "the tunnel of isolation."

While some businesses went under, others got creative. One example of innovative practices and good marketing came in July 1970 when Robert and Tina Brewer purchased Santa's Land. The deal included the old farmhouse at 646 Bellows Falls Road, six tourist cabins, a miniature golf course on the opposite side of Route 5 from the main park, and a motel just south of the park at 601 Bellows Falls Road. The park complex totaled 125 acres. The Brewer family successfully endeavored to make the park more fun for its visitors. Countless area teens had their first job experience at Santa's Land, working in the gift shop or refreshment stand, helping with the train, overseeing various animals, and dressing up as Santa's elves and nursery rhyme characters such as Little Bo Peep and the Gingerbread Man. At peak times as many as 50 people were on the payroll. Arthur H. Ruggles Jr. was Santa for over 35 years, willingly working seven days per week while

CHANGING OUR WAYS OF LIFE: 1960s–1970s

Judson Hall documented the first pleasure riders taking a spin on I-91 near Exit 4 in 1961.

the park was open from May through Christmas. He loved the children and sometimes admonished parents to remain behind his "foul" line so that he could visit with each child for as long as he chose.

The many exotic animals housed at the park over the years included a camel, pygmy goats, llamas, monkeys, macaws, swans, a lemur, an African parrot, white tail and other species of deer, and reindeer. The birth of a Lapland reindeer calf in 1974 was an unusual event for Putney. In 1975, Bob Brewer purchased eight Austrian Haflinger horses, also rare in the United States at the time. The horses arrived with their young trainer, Roy LaMonda, who together with Peter and Robert Brewer traveled near and far in two tractor trailers, exhibiting the animals at parades and fairs in both a "four-horse Haflinger hitch" and, in time, a six-horse hitch. It was quite a feat to train them to behave well in a team of four, not to mention six.

In 1972, the Brewers built an Igloo house that served as the family residence for five years. In 1978 the building was converted to the Igloo Pancake House, with a few rooms used as office space. The Igloo remained a favorite place for a Sunday brunch for 20 years.

AGRICULTURAL CHANGE

Real estate ads began to reflect the growing awareness that land could have value beyond its agricultural potential. Before the 1960s, farmland was either used or abandoned. Old timers regarded ramshackle homes and non-fertile land as useless. Many of those who abandoned their homes in the early to mid-twentieth century would never have dreamed that their property could one day have great value.

Dairy farmers listed in the 1963 Putney Business Directory inventory included Edward J. Cassidy, Norbert J. Dufresne, Robert W. Goodell, George H. Hamilton, Francis M. Marlow, Ellwyn Miller, Henry E. Phelps, Edward Temple, and Lawrence Titus from Elm Lea Farm at Putney School. Paula J. Barton specialized in poultry and eggs at what is now the corner of Fort Hill Road and Route 5. Max Bliss Jr. had a horse farm on what is now Pratt Road. Reuben O. Blood had a piggery on the River Road. William H. Darrow Sr. called himself an "orchardist" and William Darrow Jr. was operating Green Mountain Orchards. Voyle M. Hanson was listed simply as "farmer." Harlow Orchards was well established. Stanley Hollis had a poultry farm on Dusty Ridge. Alice Holway dealt in nursery stock and landscaping and ran a communal boarding house open to many of Putney's "new arrivals." Fred B. Howard was a cattle dealer who until the early 1960s kept cattle in the barn behind the Town Hall. Guy Kelsay raised beef cattle at Faraway Farm. George Mortimer was available for farming jobs. By the end of the 1970s, few of these farms remained, and those that did had adapted their methods to compete in a changing market.

Though she never had her own farm, a name associated with farming from 1944 until her death in 1972 was Carol "Hutch" Maynard. Hired by Mrs. Hinton to manage The Putney School farm and supervise the student work program, Hutch also became a milk tester for the Dairy Herd Improvement Association. Always active in town affairs, she

David Brewer drives the Austrian Haflinger horses while Cindy Lavoie and Carol Leonard go for a winter ride at Santa's Land.

106

was responsible for planting and tending a flower garden in the center triangle in Putney Village and another in front of the new Putney Central School. A vegetable garden near her home produced an abundance of vegetables which, with the help of her neighbors, were canned or frozen and donated to the Putney Central School's hot lunch program for many years.

Harlow's Sugar House and the farming experience of Don and Maddie Harlow exemplify the adaptations and ingenuity modern farmers had to exhibit in order to stay in business. Both had a lifelong love of farming and started small farming ventures when Don Harlow was 15 and Maddie Bryant was 13:

> I had all these dreams of farming and making cider. So after school, I'd say, "Maddie, you want to pick up apples?" She'd wash cider jugs. That was really our first venture. Maddie started selling cider around the corner from Harlow's Sugar House because my grandmother wouldn't let us sell it here [at the sugarhouse].

In 1957 Don and Maddie, by then a married couple with two small children, bought Harlow's Farm from Don's uncle Frank. "There was no electricity in the house or anything. By then I had two boys. We moved in here and got the power company to put in a pole and we hung a light bulb over the kitchen table. We wired the house over the winter and started sugaring the next year." The Harlows had three successful years at their farm stand before the national highway came through. "The Interstate didn't hit home until the day it opened. [Suddenly] we didn't sell anything."

The change financially devastated the farm for three years while the Harlows tried to get back on their feet. The couple showed incredible ingenuity and set some trends in what Don refers to as "entertainment farming:"

> When you owe so much money that you can't buy groceries, you got to come up with something. Nobody trained us. That's for damn sure! In January we jacked up the old sugar house and plunked it by the side of the road so people could see how it was made. That first spring, the *Christian Science Monitor* ran a front-page photo of our sugar house. My heavens! There were so many people that following Sunday that I didn't think we'd be able to move on the road.
>
> So then we started a "Pick Your Own." At the time there wasn't a farmer in Vermont who would let people walk in their strawberry fields and pick their berries. I mean you pick in a row and you pick clean and you pick the rotten ones and put them away. These people would step in a row and pick two here and see a red one over there and step over there. I told a guy once, if I wanted you to pick like that, I'd have planted them that way!

THE CLASH OF CULTURES AND COUNTER-CULTURES

Many of the social idealists at the Experiment, Putney School, and the Graduate School were members of the Society of Friends or sympathetic to Quaker beliefs of pacifism and world harmony. Morris Mitchell left the Graduate School to found the Friends World College when the program was sold to Antioch College in 1964. An official Friends meeting was established in 1965 as the Putney Preparative Meeting. The Meeting records show active involvement with the Highlander School in Tennessee, with missing civil rights workers in Mississippi, with fair housing in Vermont, and in support of local civil rights groups.

The Friends formally established in Putney at a time when superpowers were at a nuclear standoff. The Vietnam era had begun, many Americans feared a Communist conspiracy, and folks in town had vocal opinions on all sides of these issues. Votes on Town Meeting articles of the 1950s indicate that a large dissenting group was already forming and that the Republican grip on town might someday change.

The first public clash of values occurred at Putney Central School. While the school directors' report of 1966 does not mention the controversy, it filled many *Reformer* articles and the Letters to the Editor section of the newspaper. Two teachers and the principal were told in late winter of 1966 that their contracts would not be renewed, although they had not received any notification of unsatisfactory performance. In further discussions, the board did not deny that questions of religion and political belief had influenced their decision. In particular, the English and social studies teacher was criticized for her opposition to the Vietnam War and for teaching without textbooks.

To bolster his case against this type of progressive education, a school board member invited H. Vaughn Griffin of Rutland to show the PTA three short movies about the dangers of John Dewey and his progressive ideology. Dewey (1859–1952), a native Vermonter and esteemed University of Vermont alumnus, is still regarded as one of the world's most important influences in education. Griffin, according to the *Reformer*, "studied in an anti-Communist school under Fred Schwartz of Houston, Texas, head of the Christian Anti-Communist Crusade." This is important to note because all of the non-public educational institutions in Putney from the Antioch–Putney Graduate School to Putney School to the Experiment in International Living used John Dewey's philosophy of experiential learning as an inspiration for their programs. To them, the movies directly attacked their beliefs and practices.

Debate over Putney's public education continued in the letter box of the *Reformer* and at school board meetings. Letters from Putney School parents, whose children attended Putney Central, and educational leaders from Antioch-Putney challenged the School Board's actions and defended the teaching practices at Putney Central. Other concerned parents, worried that their children were subject to anti-patriotic behavior and unsuitable books like *To Kill a Mocking Bird*, criticized the education at Putney Central and spoke up publicly through letters to the editor of the *Reformer*. Meeting notes from the Putney Preparative Meeting show concern that "a segment of the community identifies Quakerism and Pacifism with Communism and feels that Quakers have a pernicious influence on children." Other staff members, dismayed by the board's actions, resigned. Finally, the School Board closed the school a week early in 1966, without notifying the teachers or the town in advance.

In retrospect, one of the teachers involved says that she now believes there is a need for new people in a community to be sensitive to the established perspectives, and that

Putney Girl Scout Troop walks down Main Street in the Memorial Day parade on May 31, 1967.

the conflict of values in 1965 and 1966 could have been reduced with a little more mutual understanding. That mutual understanding was slow to come, however. In a Windham College student paper entitled "Economic Structure in the Village of Putney," David Cohen and Polly Levin wrote in 1967, "there is a sharp division between those associated with the educational institutions and those associated with older parts of the town." The conflicts at Putney Central would soon look quite tame in comparison to the confrontations at the end of the 1960s, brought about by the public behaviors of counterculture youth and political radicals.

As a result of the conflict, some parents withdrew their children from the public school and sent them to a recently established private elementary school. The Grammar School, a day school for children in pre-school through grade eight, was founded in 1960 by a group of local families. Led by Dick Richardson and George Shumlin, the group sought to create an educational experience for their children that was both joyful and productive. The program, with its emphasis on art, music, drama, a foreign language study, reading for pleasure, and cross-country skiing was a significant alternative to the local public school program. Parents were active in all aspects of school life: most families came from Putney and many children walked or skied to school, which was located in an outbuilding on the Richardson's Aiken Road property.

In 1966, the school relocated to its present site. The Richardson family donated 60 acres of rural hillside off Hickory Ridge Road. The grounds included woods, a stream, a small frog pond, open meadow, playgrounds and athletic fields, as well as ski/bike trails. George Heller designed the main building. This original plan provided for a student body of 50 to 60 students in five small classrooms, a design that emphasized the value of small class sizes and low student teacher ratio. The Grammar School eventually expanded to the adjoining property and enrolled 117 students in 2002.

Throughout the later 1960s and the 1970s, Putney served as a magnet for the counterculture. The area was steeped in the sixties drug culture and well known for its cultivation of marijuana. Windham College attracted speakers such as anti-war activist and baby authority Dr. Benjamin Spock, a youthful and idealistic faculty recruited from high caliber universities, and students like Bill Powell who wrote the Anarchist Cookbook. Windham developed a reputation as a college for draft dodgers, although a look at remaining records shows almost as many women graduated as men. College students now dominated the small town center and some locals found their actions and appearance increasingly offensive.

Overt acts of confrontation on both sides of a political and cultural divide increased tensions to a boiling point. Two episodes stand out in people's minds: the makeshift barbershop erected in the center of town and the summer of the Free Farm. The first involved long-haired "hippies," who appeared to locals to be extremely dirty and disheveled. Arguments of the time about length of hair and type of dress took an old-style New England twist in July of 1969 when some townspeople erected a pillory near the center of town and placed a bathtub and a red and white barbershop pole next to it. As "hippies" passed by they were harassed and threatened with sheep shears. The "barbershop" incident was reported in the newspaper through a vivid photo with caption.

The Free Farm is a longer story. Artist John Douglas "came up to Putney for a ride" with a friend in March 1965, having just gotten out of the army. He and his friends stopped at a real estate office and the realtor told them about a farm that had just come out of probate court. John bought it for $18,000, fixed it up, and left for New York City to help start Newsreel, a radical film cooperative that produced movies about politics and social change. After finishing a film in North Vietnam in 1969, a group of the Newsreel folks decided to come to Putney to live instead of returning to New York. Using John's farmhouse and property, they established the Red Clover Collective.

Red Clover became a base of operations for state and national political activism, watched by the FBI and harassed by locals, until a dramatic confrontation in the fall of 1970 scattered members to other places. Although the name remains, the current owners of Red Clover were not associated with its earlier history. As part of its political strategy, the original Red Clover group recruited from local communes and college campuses. A Putney resident and former Free Farm member recalls the events surrounding the establishment and destruction of the Free Farm:

> We [a group of college students, street people, itinerate Hippies and such] asked the president of the college if we could start a community garden in the spring of 1970 on some college property near The Red House on Route 5. The school agreed to let us use the field and we dubbed ourselves "The Free Farm." As part of work on the garden, we'd have Sunday meetings and cookouts. Dozens of people would come. We'd make a big pot of vegetable stew and rice. Politicos would come down and talk radical politics. We played conga drums, howled, took our clothes off, stuff like that.

A lot of friction developed with the more conservative, local people and with the college. As the school year approached, they got interested in getting us off the land. We welcomed this confrontation as the fulfillment of some of our radical fantasies.

On freshman orientation week-end there was a barbecue on campus. The college got the state police to come down and cordon off the field where our garden was, but it was too large an area, so they only blocked the road frontage. We had flags and banners and all of a sudden came rushing in on the field from the woods and reclaimed the garden. Then, we marched en masse down to Windham College to let the incoming class know that we were here.

Townspeople observing thought, what's the deal here? No one is handling this out-of-control situation. They waited two Sundays and then gathered a convoy of pick-up trucks, vigilante style, and drove onto the vegetable garden. If our fantasy was Hippie Revolution, you could say theirs was Frontier Justice. A couple dozen of us went over to talk and the guys in the pick-ups thought that we were coming for a confrontation. They pointed to their rifles and then jumped from their pick-up trucks and beat the crap out of us. It went pretty fast. Before I knew it, I was at the hospital getting my head stitched up. After the beating, people were still on the field. Then, some communards went back home, got weapons of their own and brought them up to the field. There wasn't any shooting, but it seems as though it was close.

Years later it was much easier for me to see what an intrusion Windham

The Colegium chorus practiced at Newman Hall in the 1960s under the direction of George Soulos.

111

College must have been to Putney. It literally took over the town. Now, I get annoyed listening to the Landmark kids drive their cars up my road on a Saturday night. And that is pretty minor in comparison to what we were doing. I felt like we were quite arrogant. Which is too bad because I still believe that a lot of our ideas were good.

Our differences were ideological. And what does that really mean in terms of day to day existence? When I came back to Putney a couple of years later, I really appreciated just being a carpenter and was more aware of what I had in common with townspeople. I realized that I had asked a lot of people in terms of my behavior and my appearance. Our ideas are still different, but we coexist. It's heartening. In the end, the small acts of everyday life have been powerful.

ENTERTAINMENT, RECREATION, AND HERITAGE

Seeking to revive the town spirit generated by the Bicentennial celebrations, a similar celebration was held in 1963 to mark Putney's 210th anniversary. This event was co-sponsored by the newly formed Putney Historical Society and the Putney Civic Association. On Friday, August 9, an opening tea and art exhibit at the Earlham Gallery on Route 5 was followed by an "Old Fashioned Square Dance" at Pierce's Hall with Ted Glabach, caller. Saturday the 10th, a "Merchant's Carnival" was held all day on the Windham College Green on Route 5 (site of Chittenden Bank and Windward Performance Products in 2003). There was a Baby Carriage Parade and a Decorated Bicycle Parade with the Putney Junior Police. The day included a puppet show with Peter Shumann and an auction with auctioneer Jeffrey Campbell. Putney musicians

This photo of downtown Putney from 1969 shows the growth that took place in the 1960s that would continue into the 1970s and 1980s.

offered a musical evening at Putney Central School. On Sunday there were special church services and in the afternoon, open house programs at the Experiment, The Putney School, Putney Graduate School, and Windham College. An ad placed in the program by Campbell Greene & Co. of Brattleboro congratulated Putney and added: "May you never have parking meters."

With a new museum as a public attraction, the Putney Historical Society, founded in 1959, began a formal effort to preserve the town's heritage and educate its citizenry. Inez Harlow maintained the dual role of town clerk and town historian. By the mid-1970s she groomed Laura Heller and Elaine Dixon to take over the reins as museum curators. They are still quick to say that it took two people to fill Inez's shoes. In celebration of the country's Bicentennial, the Historical Society prepared a traveling slide show to teach school children about Putney's history. With funds from the National Council on the Humanities, Geordie Heller was able to print photographs from the Society's extensive glass plate negative collections before they deteriorated beyond repair. Thanks to this effort, the Putney Historical Society owns an excellent photo collection of late nineteenth and early twentieth century images.

The sons and grandsons of the baseball players of the 1930s kept the tradition going strong until the late 1960s when softball took over. The Senior and Junior baseball teams formed in Putney in 1948 were reorganized by the early 1960s as part of the newly-formed Putney Athletic Club. In 1965 the "A.C.s" won the West River Valley League championship and it seemed that they would be around for a long time. Aggressive fund-raisers, the club held Hunter's Balls during deer season and "really packed 'em in." They sold many raffle tickets and some years cleared in excess of $2,000 to support their team as well as a basketball program for boys at the Community Center. With proceeds, they built a new backstop, announcing booth, and dugouts at Cooper Field on Sand Hill Road, installed electricity, and built a fence behind the outfield. In 1965 they reported themselves as "one of the best equipped and uniformed baseball teams in Vermont," having spent $1,095.51 on uniforms and equipment. In 1965 and 1966 they sponsored the National Baseball Congress State Tournament. But the West River Valley League dissolved in 1968 and Putney baseball ended abruptly—at least for the next three decades. The A.C.s disbanded in the late 1970s and not until 1987 would another organization, the Recreation League, take their place.

From 1967 through 1971, Putney softball teams belonged to the Brattleboro league and had to travel to Brattleboro for all games. Harris Coomes, long time hometown baseball and basketball player and organizer, became an official umpire in 1970 and helped to organize the Putney Softball League in 1972. The old baseball diamond on Cooper's Field was permanently remodeled for softball. The backstop was rotated so that it no longer faced northwest but more southwest. Much dirt was trucked in to fill in the bank and expand the area east of left field. Fund-raising that took place to provide lights for night playing was to be in vain. Though enough was raised to install the lights, there wasn't enough money coming in from team dues to pay for electricity. When softball was at its peak in the 1970s, former Windham students and native "Putney boys" played on the same wild and crazy team called The Master Batters, forming friendships that would largely erase the initial distinction between them.

113

Though much work was done in the early 1960s on the "East Putney Puddle" on East Putney Brook just west of River Road, there remained a need for a good place to swim. As the idea of building a town pool materialized, a special Town Meeting was held in 1967. Voters approved, 67 to 19, an article allowing the newly formed Recreation Board to purchase a parcel of land on Westminster West road for the construction of a new pool at an estimated cost of $4,276.37. Volunteers were on hand to dig and Earl Stockwell manned the bulldozer. Lined with cardboard, the pool became a much-enjoyed addition to the town's recreational resources for the next 35 years.

Deer season was an important local tradition and form of recreation. For many hunters it was less about killing a deer and more about the chance to experience some solitude in the forest—to walk in the footsteps of earlier inhabitants who had stalked their food with ancient weapons. But a century and a half of freedom to hunt at will for food and sport had made it necessary to protect the remaining deer population by limiting the activity to a short season in the fall, thereby making it an annual ritual more than an act of survival.

As long as the older hunters alive today can remember, it was an accepted fact that a man could be expected to take at least the first week of deer season off from work to hunt or join his buddies at deer camp. According to one such long-time hunter, "In those days [the 1950s and 1960s] it was bumper to bumper on Hickory Ridge and Dusty Ridge" which were known as superior hunting areas. Restaurants, cabins, and motels did a huge business throughout Windham County, which had the highest deer kill rate in the state during that era.

This was also big business for many towns in Vermont and particularly in Putney when Ernest Parker was the town clerk. As his personality and willingness to accommodate attracted so many out-of-state hunters to stop and buy licenses from him, (especially after the opening of I-91 with its handy Exit 4), he expanded his office hours—eventually pulling all-nighters. He hired many assistant clerks to help him, sometimes as many as six or seven at once. During 1966, his last year in his office at 101 Main Street, he and his assistants shattered state records by selling 4,920 hunting and fishing licenses, and turning over a total of $62,943 to the State of Vermont. The night before deer season was an almost carnival atmosphere at Mr. Parker's office where the money came in so fast it was simply stuffed into large paper grocery bags until morning when it could be counted and banked. But, as many of Putney's new residents built homes in the remoter areas of town, increasingly posted land and the lure of larger deer in northern Vermont caused hunting in Putney to practically cease by the early 1970s.

Throughout the 1960s, 1970s, and into the 1980s the Community Center flourished, supported by annual "opportunity sales," proceeds from dances, and some help from the town. In 1964, the first year that the Town Report included an annual report for the Center, President Shirley Ellis reported that the Junior Police, Boy Scouts, Cub Scouts, Girl Scouts, and Brownies all met weekly. Basketball was played every afternoon, five days per week. Other activities sponsored by the center that year included a Halloween party, a Christmas Workshop, Roller-skating, Skiing lessons, a Sugar-on-Snow party, cooking classes for girls, 12 different Walt Disney films (each with attendance of 75–80 people), and occasional Friday night dances for the grade school children. Private groups held three wedding receptions and numerous showers. In 1969 a program was started in

The Master Batters pose for a group picture in the late 1970s.

conjunction with the Bellows Falls YMCA, opening a teen room three afternoons per week and on Friday and Saturday nights, continuing well into the 1980s. Pool, ping-pong, chess, checkers, and a jukebox were provided. The YMCA hired a coordinator and Windham College's Circle K Club provided student assistants. Winning the 1971 YMCA championship for Putney in ping pong were Deb Derrig and Torrey Ellis; in caroms the champion was Darcy Washburn.

In 1973, the Community Center recreated the old field days that had been held in the 1940s and 1950s and introduced the "Fun Fest." Cooper's field was the scene of an all-day affair, preceded by a large parade. Minnie Coomes was crowned "Queen of Putney" in appreciation for her many years of dedication to the town's youth. Horse-drawings, barbecued chicken, horseshoe competitions, softball, and other games brought back a taste of the old days. The event was repeated annually for 12 years.

Adult dances were held during the 1970s and early 1980s at Newman Hall. New on the scene in the early seventies was a promising young group who called themselves the Green Mountain Boys. Bruce and Barry Stockwell and their cousins Doug and Tim Harlow began wowing audiences with their renditions of bluegrass and country rock. The group accepted engagements all over New England. Later, Doug and Tim left the group to pursue other ventures while Bruce and Barry made a career performing as The Stockwell Brothers band.

In the summer, Putney Bicycle Club drew a crowd of bikers for racing events organized by the West Hill Bike Shop. The club welcomed all to join whether they were beginners, "hot shots," or "slow pokes." In the winter Putney School continued to make a name

The Brattleboro Reformer *printed this Judson Hall photo c. 1964, showing work on the "East Putney Puddle."*

for itself in the world of cross-country skiing. Student Peter Caldwell won the 1972 title of Vermont High School Skimeister at the championship meet in Middlebury. His teammate Bill Koch had not yet reached his potential but in 1978 made Putney very proud by bringing home an Olympic silver medal.

EXPANSION OF PUBLIC SERVICES

Putney had its share of radicalism in the 1960s and 1970s, but gradual and more moderate changes ultimately had the larger impact. John A. (Jack) Wallace, founder of the School for International Training, and moderator of the Putney Town Meetings from 1957 to 1983, described the development of Putney from his vantage:

> When I first became Moderator, the town had a population of about 1,200 people. Within that population the dominant group had been born right here in Vermont. It was a conservative group in the sense of wanting to conserve—or preserve—the character of the town. It was also a group favoring economy. . . . As I-91 pushed steadily northward the nature of the population slowly shifted to produce a town majority of newcomers. Many had moved here from urban and suburban communities in which they had become accustomed to a wide variety of services and institutions paid for by public funds. They wanted similar services here in Putney and as the 60s moved into the 70s, their voices became the dominant ones. . . . Putney became a "bedroom community," for which we have to thank—or blame—Senator George Aiken, who lobbied his fellow Republican, President Eisenhower, to include an I-91 exit for Aiken's home town.

Most of the public services those newcomers desired are common place today: a day care center, public kindergarten, a better school lunch program, improved roads, a water and sewer system, and a sidewalk from the village to the Central School. Yet it took several tries to convince a majority of voters to agree to spend the necessary tax dollars. The nursery school was never approved, the sidewalk would have to wait another 20 years, the water system 30 years, but public kindergarten, first requested in 1967, was finally approved in 1974: 187 yes to 186 no. The opponents rallied and attempted to reverse the decision but in 1975, kindergarten approval prevailed with 235 voting yes and 226 voting no.

Plans for Community, Inc. began in the late 1960s through an action group sponsored by the Federated Church. At the last minute the original start-up was cancelled because parents could not afford the $18 per week fee. Inspired by a women's liberation lecture at Windham College, Mal Herbert organized a day care center as part of her graduate work-project at Antioch-Putney in 1970–1971. To lower expenses, Windham College allocated Work-Study funds to student aides and Antioch-Putney supplied graduate interns. The Community Nursery School Board loaned money to support the day care on a short term basis. Ten mothers and two fathers staffed the center as part of a child-care collective. Ivy Darrow guided the finances for decades.

Eventually, the group received state licensing and state and federal funding to subsidize operating expenses. When Mal took a job with Follow-Through in Brattleboro, Ramona Carter took her place as director. After Ramona's departure, Eva Mondon and Faith Pepe changed the governance structure so that the day care center was run as a workers collective. The position of director was switched to one of coordinator. All salaries for coordinators and child care workers were on par. The Center switched locations many times before settling into its current location, offered by Connie St. John in 1974. Community Day Care won gradual support from the town, starting with a $50 appropriation approved at Town Meeting in 1970.

The need for a town sewer system had become increasingly obvious as some of the older houses in the center of town were converted for use as dormitories for Windham College. Some had no septic tanks whatsoever. Town Health Officer Dr. John Houpis specifically mentioned these buildings when he spoke at Town Meeting in 1968 about the health hazards of having sewerage draining "right into the middle of town." He had condemned two such buildings the previous day. Serious planning begun in 1965 finally reached the construction phase in 1975. At last, in July of 1976, 101 users were hooked up to the completed system.

Selectman Donald Harlow, then board chairman, first expressed the need for professional assistance with governance at the beginning of Town Meeting in 1968. The "some six hundred odd Federal programs where money is available, a "college which is now nearly as large as Putney," and other pressing issues had become overwhelming to the three-person board charged with the responsibility of running a growing town. There had been some talk of increasing the board to five persons but relief came at last, thanks to the Federal Emergency Employment Act of 1971 that allowed the Selectmen to hire Alan Benjamin as administrative assistant. The position was continued the following year using Revenue Sharing money. Benjamin left to work for another town in 1974 and was replaced by Stephen Fitch, who became the first town manager in 1976 when the town agreed to adopt the new system of government permanently. John Bagge, former Putney Central School principal, took over the position in 1979.

Law enforcement became a considerable problem in the late 1960s, with the two constables Bill Graham and Malcolm (Mack) Jones Jr. dealing with a myriad of issues including traffic, parking, controlled substances, criminal activity, and protests. Until the late 1960s there were no two-way radios, and the constables would be alerted by a light outside town hall, which would indicate that they should call in to see what the problem was. The majority of voters refused to fund participation in the Windham County Sheriff's Department until 1970. By then, Bill Graham had become county sheriff, a position he held for over 30 years.

As society became more conscious about pollution, the legislature churned out new laws and regulations. Putney's old dump did not comply and by 1969, Putney was forced to create a land fill dump. By 1975, the rules were even stricter and, after suffering the expense of a large underground fire, the town gave in to continuing pressure from the state and made the decision to close the dump for good, contracting to use the Brattleboro Landfill. As the town had just used Revenue Sharing money to purchase the 999-year lease of the 26-acre parcel on which the dump was situated in 1974, it was chosen as the site for the new town garage built in 1977. Taking advantage of $137,280 received from the Federal Economic Development Administration, the garage only cost the taxpayers $1,000. The following year the EDA provided Putney with $199,000 for improvements to Putney Central School and $75,000 to upgrade the fire station.

Putney was slow to warm to the concept of zoning. Perhaps the arrival of the college convinced the voters to give it a chance as interim zoning was adopted in 1969 after three years of work by the Planning Commission. Actual zoning regulations were approved in September 1971 by a vote of 244 to 162. Interim zoning for flood hazard areas was adopted in 1975, qualifying the town for federally subsidized flood hazard insurance. A revised set of zoning regulations passed in 1978 by a clearer majority of 281 to 116.

When a new library was constructed on the corner of Route 5 and Old Route 5 in 1967, the town finally made use of the old school district #1 property that voters had refused to sell way back in 1906. The town hall space the library vacated was then converted to town office space. A new vault was completed in 1973. Retiring Town Clerk Inez Harlow barely had time to enjoy the new Xerox 914 copier purchased in 1976 to make the job of recording deeds easier. Prior to the $2,740 purchase, Mrs. Harlow had carefully copied each deed and document by hand—as had all the Town Clerks before her.

Wishing to make a contribution to the town, the Lions Club sponsored a contest for a town logo design in 1979. The winner was Sacha Hewitt, who drew the sketch that now hangs as a plaque above the front door of the town hall. The logo appears on all official town stationery.

As the 1970s drew to a close, Putney was a very different place from what it had been 20 years earlier. Some felt that too many decisions had been taken from the hands of residents by state and federal mandates, and through the acceptance of substantial grants from Revenue Sharing and similar programs. After passing through the turmoil of the 1960s, it certainly was no longer a sleepy little community of self-sufficient farms. Indeed, as the Selectmen pointed out in 1979, of the 336 votes cast at Town Meeting, only 170 actually owned land in Putney. And even those 336 votes represented a very small percentage of the total number of eligible voters, seeming evidence of citizen apathy. On the other hand, the modernization of Putney now provided its citizens with many of the services and amenities expected by most Americans. Were Putney voters apathetic, or simply content? Times had changed and Putney had changed with them.

The Green Mountain Boys (Doug Harlow, Bruce Stockwell, Tim Harlow, Barry Nutbrown, and Barry Stockwell) are shown here at a Memorial Day program at the Town Hall in 1969. Two of the group continue to please audiences 34 years later as The Stockwell Brothers.

8. Adjusting to a New Era: 1980s

The national shift of priorities during the Reagan Era meant less federal funding for Putney and a need for greater efforts by town leaders to revitalize the town's economic base. Educational innovation played a major role in this process, as did the development of an organized crafts movement and the appearance of several new businesses. Town spending, and taxes, continued to grow rapidly, but somehow Putney remained an attractive destination for folks seeking the slower pace of life in Vermont. New homes were built, and their new residents contributed to an ever-changing mix that had come to typify Putney.

Greenwood School and Landmark College

By the late 1970s, Putney had two vacant educational properties, left by the move of the Experiment to Brattleboro and the dissolution of Windham College. The first property to exchange educational hands was that held by the Experiment in International Living. Looking for a location to found their own school, Tom and Andrea Scheidler came to Putney and discovered that the former Experiment campus was on the market. They bought the property in the fall of 1978 and founded the Greenwood School for 9- to 14-year-old boys with learning differences. Former teachers at Linden Hill School in Massachusetts, the Scheidlers came to believe that students with specific learning differences did not need medicating in order to learn. "We worked with young boys with very high intelligence who had difficulty with one aspect of learning," Andrea Scheidler said in a Putney Historical Society interview with Stuart Strothman. "Not being good at reading should not be used as a measure of intelligence. These children are creative; they have incredible memories; they take the 360-degree view. They are so smart." The Scheidlers fostered their vision of education until they retired in June 1999 after 21 years at the helm. The school still operates with a dedicated staff whose teaching approach honors the individual talents of all learners and offers much individual instruction.

Once it became clear that Windham College was gone for good, community leaders began an effort to attract organizations to the empty campus, both to revitalize the economy and to save the campus from becoming an empty, hulking bit of unwanted real estate. As the months passed, Putney citizens attended several meetings and in 1980, approved zoning the campus as a commercial site. By 1982, various corporations were toying with the idea of developing the site into an industrial conference center. A man from Texas even proposed a refugee center for "Asians," an appealing idea until it was revealed to be a scam. Though it was not generally known at that time, Selectman Peter Shumlin and Town Manager John Bagge were discussing a new option with Charles Drake, president of the Landmark School in Beverly, Massachusetts. Drake's high school specialized in students with learning disabilities and he had long sought to create a college with that same focus.

Even as these talks were proceeding, still another option emerged, suggested by the major lien-holder of the bankrupt college property, the federal government. It was revealed that the Federal Bureau of Prisons had eminent domain over the property and had decided that the site would be a good location for a new minimum security prison. A group of Putney town leaders including Ian Eddy, Doug Harlow, John Bagge, and Fred Breunig flew to Allentown, Pennsylvania to view Allenwood, a minimum security facility there. The atmosphere in Putney was charged, with many people opposing the idea, believing the "feds" would try to railroad the citizens and force the prison on a resistant citizenry.

A panel of federal representatives presented its proposal at a special Town Meeting in March 1983. Attendance was higher than at any previous Town Meeting and many people spoke. Some doubted there would actually be a vote, although John Bagge reported afterward that the federal representatives intended to abide by the voters' wishes all along. Maryann Parrott stood up on two occasions and asked clearly, "Can we vote?" Near the end of the meeting, then Brattleboro resident Wayne Lauden asked if he could address the meeting. Once granted permission to speak, Wayne turned to look at the audience and announced that he had been a prisoner at Allenwood, serving a sentence for draft resistance during the Vietnam War. Wayne Lauden spoke of his friendship with prison guards whose attitude toward Allenwood was that, while the prisoners left after a few years, they were sentenced to be there for life. Wayne's statement added a stark reality to the picture being painted by the federal officials. This, combined with the revelation that the prison system could change the designation from minimum to maximum security at any time without having to come back to the town for permission, persuaded townspeople that the prison option would not bring the kinds of jobs Putney residents sought. Peter Shumlin then announced that another viable alternative existed: a school was interested in obtaining the property.

When the vote did take place, the proposal to allow a prison at the former Windham College campus was soundly defeated, 536 to 186. John Bagge resumed negotiations with Drake before the night was over, and several local people stepped forward to buy the property until Landmark could purchase it. Once the town settled its claims against the Windham College Corporation for $34,000, the entire Windham Campus (except for its Fine Arts Building) passed smoothly to a newly created Landmark College, and a new chapter in Putney's educational history began.

Drake was intimately involved with the establishment of Landmark College and staffed it with many veteran educators from the Landmark School and a few former Windham College professors. It was the first of its kind, providing an intense learning experience for students with a history of difficulty learning in mainstream educational programs. Among the early leaders of the school were Jim Olivier, founding president; and his wife Carolyn Olivier, director of admissions, and later co-author of the book *Learning to Learn*. Along with Geof Gaddis, chief financial officer; Jim Baucom, academic dean; Jeroo Eduljee, academic director; former Windham librarian Bob Rhodes; and a team of caring faculty, the Oliviers created a stable, supportive, yet highly demanding program for students. The school grew into the only accredited college in the country designed exclusively for students of average to superior intellectual potential with dyslexia, attention deficit hyperactivity disorder (AD/HD), or specific learning disabilities. A strict attendance policy, nearly five hours of tutorial sessions weekly, heavy emphasis on study skills and language learning, a student/teacher ratio of 3:1 or lower, and a dry campus all set this institution apart from any other, and enrollment grew slowly but steadily.

One after another, dormitories and classroom buildings were repaired and renovated and the campus came to life again. To further beautify it, reduce maintenance costs, and make a clear break with the past, the school decided to remove the white paint that had been specified for the entire campus by Edward Durrell Stone, restoring the buildings to a beautiful natural brick.

Since their founding, both The Greenwood School and Landmark College have been on the cutting edge of education, employing increased educational services and new styles of teaching for students with difficulty learning in traditional settings. With these two institutions, Putney gained national recognition for leadership in the education of students with learning differences.

NEW ERA IN TOWN GOVERNMENT

The 1980s saw trends in town government that reflected earlier changes in population and demography. Just as the "revenue sharing" of the Nixon era dissipated, the new demands of a larger town population for such things as road surfacing, maintenance, and the fire department increased. A major problem the fire department and chief Bruce Howard faced in 1983, besides needing a new truck, was that state regulations temporarily prohibited the cleaning of silt from Sacketts Brook dam, where the fire trucks needed regular access to clear water. The issue wasn't resolved until 1988. In 1981 road foreman Leighton Cleverly attended a Mack truck maintenance program, and before the decade was over the town was taking advantage of a buyback program for Mack trucks, which has saved considerable money and need for repair, following a regular schedule of truck replacement.

Newly elected governor Madeline Kunin was present at the 1979 Town Meeting. During her six years in office, state spending on education and human services nearly doubled and a corresponding increase occurred in Putney. The various economic issues wrestled with in that period led the Selectmen to declare a fiscal crisis, and to exclude the human service organizations from the town budget in 1983 and 1984.

In response, a number of human service organizations, including the Council on Aging, the Putney Community Center, Public Health Nursing, Mental Health Services of Southern Vermont, the Putney Recreation Club, the Women's Crisis Center, Rescue Inc., the Youth Services Bureau, and Hotline, asked for a vote by Australian Ballot. All of them

After less than a decade in full operation, the Windham College campus stood vacant. This image, showing cows at pasture, was part of a series of publicity photos taken for the college in the mid-1970s.

had their requested contribution approved. In 1985, Thomas Ehrenberg's first year as moderator, an $11, 865 budget for human service organizations was approved. None came from revenue sharing, all of it came from local taxes. This increase in services, approved by a majority of the voters, was characteristic of the changing style of government that increased budgets at the state and the local levels. For instance, the 1988 Town Meeting approved $5,000 to create the position of recreation coordinator.

However, the really big increases came in educational spending. The school budget of $446,542 in 1979 increased by 1987 to $797,385, reflecting increased enrollment, various small construction projects, and a national trend toward increased educational services. The few voters who attended the 1987 Town Meeting approved a tax increase of 23.7 percent. Attendance at Town Meeting was very low that year, with only a small percentage of the community deciding the way their money was going to be spent. A proposal to direct legislators to reject any state-imposed property tax produced a tie vote of 45, and a resolution to hold Town Meetings in handicap-accessible places was defeated, with 14 in favor and 26 against! At the end of the meeting Mabel Gray wanted to see the list and investigate why more voters weren't present at Town Meeting, where such important decisions were made.

Considerable debate developed in Town Meetings about whether to continue to use the county sheriff for law enforcement. The town came closest to change in 1981, when the townspeople upheld the contract by a vote of 235 to 233. During all of this time Bill Graham remained as county sheriff, bringing considerable professionalism to the position.

Officers who applied for county positions were required to have a high school diploma and criminal justice training from the State of Vermont. There was also a psychological exam, a record check, and even a polygraph, which is not usually required in Vermont. Then there was a personal interview involving the sheriff and a local citizen from one or another town served by the sheriff. Dave Hannum Jr. and Mike Muscat of Putney both served on this committee on different occasions. Many of the leaders in the department, such as Graham, Mac Jones, Henry Farnum, and John Melvin, underwent a 12-week FBI training program in Washington, D.C., taking advantage of some of the best police training available in the United States. To increase awareness of speeding, in the early 1990s the Windham Sheriff's Department was the first in the state to acquire the roadside trailers that compare drivers' actual speeds to the speed limit.

The general issue of Putney air and water quality was at the forefront of town politics throughout the 1980s. In response to the new environmental regulations, Putney Paper created a series of lagoons in the 1970s for recycling wastewater to avoid drainage into the Connecticut River. However, the lagoons created an unpleasant odor in much of the village district, and the town eventually got the mill to clean the lagoons, route secondary sludge to their landfill, install further equipment to recycle water, and use odor-consuming chemicals. The selectboard was pleased with the mill's cooperation with the town's desire to reduce odor and still adhere to environmental regulations. In 1988 the mill received a plaque for resolving the problem.

Landmark College was founded on the former Windham campus in 1983 and welcomed its first students in 1985. These students are from the graduating class of 2002.

124

BUSINESSES: NEW AND OLD

The closing of Windham College caused a temporary lull in business activity in town, until optimistic entrepreneurs slowly reappeared. Following the death of Betsy Mellen in 1983, the Mellen's store building was eventually sold to Neil Madow, who opened Silver Forest of Vermont as the retail outlet for the Silver Forest jewelry company located in Rockingham. Shirley Lockerby and Carol Carbone decided to take a chance and establish Putney's first beauty salon, opening Shear Madness for business in October 1985, on the second floor of the former Perfectionist Chapel building at 128 Main Street, directly over the Putney Diner. Shirley became the sole owner in 1988. Putney's second beauty salon, Deb's Hair and Wig Shop, was opened by Deb Fitzpatrick just two years later at 27 Houghton Brook Road. Karla Hurwitz opened the Putney Fruit Company restaurant in the building where the Perfectionists once maintained a grocery store. There were now seven places one could have a sit-down meal in Putney: the Putney Inn, the Putney Summit Restaurant, the Putney Diner, the Putney Fruit Company, Mountain Paul's, the Putney General Store, and Curtis's B-B-Q, ("America's Seventh Wonder of the World").

Carol Berry and Jonathan Altman began making all natural, gourmet pasta in their renovated barn on Hickory Ridge Road in 1983. The company, which they named Putney Pasta, started in a 4,500-square-foot space with only three workers. Later, as the company grew, it relocated to a 42,000-square-foot building in Chester, Vermont. Having built brand equity, Carol and Jonathan retained the company name once they moved. Putney Pasta has grown over the years to employ 30 people in the pasta plant and expanded its services to include a restaurant as well.

Claire Wilson, along with Libby Mills, David Ritchie, and Diana Wahle, founded the Green Mountain Spinnery in 1981, refurbishing an old Mobil station across from the Putney Inn. Also in the 1980s, Graeme King constructed King Boat Works just beyond the Spinnery, further out on what is now known as Brick Yard Lane, becoming a neighbor to the West Hill Shop and architect George Heller. Although this cluster of businesses pays taxes to Dummerston, most of the owners are Putney residents and are therefore included in the town's history. Since an adjustment in the 1800s, when 50 acres originally allocated to the town of Dummerston were annexed to Putney, the town line between Putney and Dummerston has followed the line of Putney Landing Road down to the river. After the construction of Interstate 91, the northeast corner of Dummerston was cut off from the rest of that town, accessible only from this border road in Putney.

Another novel business established in the 1980s was Hickory Ridge House, a bed and breakfast in the large brick house built in 1808 by Theophilus and Annis Crawford and occupied by that family until the early twentieth century. Phil Chase, brother of the founder of The Putney School, and his wife Helen lived in it after World War II, and for a brief time it was the president's house for Windham College. A family from California, the Brostroms, opened it as a B&B in 1984 after extensive renovations, but decided for health reasons to sell it in 1986 to Steve Anderson and Jacquie Walker, who ran it into the twenty-first century. It was sold in 2002 to innkeepers Cory and Miriam Greenspan.

Culture and the Arts

Craftspeople have always played a part in the life of Putney, as in most New England villages. Blacksmiths and woodworkers, weavers, knitters, potters, and quilt makers made useful and beautiful objects that filled the needs of everyday life while adding aesthetic pleasure to house or wearer. Although a small group of families such as the Smeads have lived in Putney for generations, making baskets, turning wood, and doing other handicrafts, Putney's growing reputation in the arts attracted a large group of artisans to the area in the 1970s and 1980s.

The Arts and Crafts Movement of the late nineteenth century encouraged a new appreciation of handmade objects and influenced the thinking of designers and decorators well into the twentieth century. Although fairs such as the one at Sunapee, New Hampshire had showcased and sold handcrafted goods to connoisseurs for years, it wasn't until the 1960s that Americans began to see crafts as a highly desirable possession or profession. Turning away from conventional jobs and 9–5 office hours, many college graduates with a creative bent and others who wished to live a self-actualizing life in a rural setting turned to the potter's wheel or the lathe to fulfill their dreams and struggle to earn their living.

As word spread through the greater crafts community that Putney—accessible yet rural—was a setting that provided attractive locations for studios and the companionship of other like-minded people, more and more migrated to the hills and valleys of Putney. By 1981, the Putney Artisans Directory listed over 100 names. Many of these people were known for their exhibits at big, juried craft shows. As respect for fine crafts work and the desire to own it grew in the society at large, the name Putney became increasingly associated with professional crafts. Both residents and visitors in search of beautiful objects to take home could find a cherry table by Richard Bissell, ornamental tiles by Carol Keiser, or perhaps a large decorative pottery piece by Ken Pick.

Inspired by her research for a paper about the craftspeople of Putney for the Fortnightly Club in 1981, Margot Torrey, a woodcut printmaker and organizer, put out an invitation to craftspeople for a get-together. At subsequent potluck suppers, more were welcomed into the circle and an informal organization, the Putney Artisans' League, was formed. It was dedicated to an exchange of information of mutual interest, to projects such as a directory of artisans and, eventually, to planning an all-Putney Artisans' Festival. The Selectboard was successfully petitioned to allow the Town Hall and grounds to be used and the first festival, enhanced by food vendors and entertained by Fred Breunig, Alan Blood, and other musicians, took place in September 1981. It had several goals: to show the local community what was being made here in studios hidden away in barns and houses, to enjoy and celebrate each others' work, and to sell the work to local and visiting buyers.

Thus, with the help and participation of Bill Caldwell, Dale Good, Ian and Jenny Eddy, Adam and Debbi Wetzel, Ken Pick, Judy Hodson, Bob Burch, Deborah Bump, Lilli Crites, Nora and Jim Zellmer, Elizabeth Lewis, Robert Olson, and many others, the crafts community introduced itself to Putney. It was a festive and successful event and was repeated in 1982 and 1983.

When Ian and Jenny Eddy (blacksmithing) and Carol and David Mischke (pottery) began joining forces to have Christmas Open-House and Seconds Sales, the need to add more craftspeople to the list of Open Studios arose, and the seeds of the Putney Holiday Craft Tour were planted. Although it was begun as a hospitable commercial venture, many of the craftspeople wanted to demonstrate how their work was made in the setting where it happens. Celebrating the process in such a manner gave the public not just interesting entertainment, but a new respect for the value of the finished product.

It was the aesthetic and educational aspects, as much as the commercial one, that provided the stimulus to keep it going. Each spring Margot Torrey called together the resident craftspeople to form a group to repeat the experience. Sharing the many tasks involved, they produced the tour of crafts studios in Putney that eventually became a very successful enterprise and a model for the Vermont Crafts Council and many other communities in Vermont and elsewhere. 2003 marked its 25th year.

Over the years, the Crafts Tour affected Putney businesses as well, which in turn contributed funds to publicize the tour. Several commercial outlets for local craft work appeared over the years. In the 1970s, a crafts cooperative was organized by Bill Northey, painter and sculptor, to sell local wares. From 1976–1996 Margot Torrey's Putney Woodshed Crafts Gallery offered local craftspeople a place to show and sell their work in a barn on Main Street. The old Grange Hall at the bottom of Kimball Hill was purchased and renovated by Caleb Kissling, who turned the ground floor into his cabinet making

The photo shows one of the maintenance crew members as he helped to build a new #1 machine at the Putney Paper Mill. The crew tore out the old machine that used wooden bearings and replaced it with an entirely new system, built from scratch.

Ian Eddy, who helped to start the Crafts Tour, is shown here working in his blacksmith shop.

workshop. Subsequently Bill Price transformed the space into an art gallery, and then in 1986 Doris Fredericks established the Putney Clay School there, as a showroom and teaching facility. Linda MacMillan was to be found at her spinning wheel at a shop in the center of the village where clothing of precious yarn was available. Sharing the shop, Judy Zemel sat at her loom weaving scarves, stoles, and rugs she offered for sale.

The Green Mountain Spinnery has processed wool from New England fleece since 1981, but also markets sweaters and patterns designed by Putney artists to go with its array of many-colored yarns. Craftspeople like glassblower Bob Burch worked with the schools, offered workshops, or took on apprentices. Burch and others open their studios at other times of the year for demonstrations and sales.

All this activity helped to develop Putney's reputation as an artistic community, which has in turn added to the number of travelers who come to Putney for its offerings of craft work, music, and dance. Many residents have been involved in dance and music these past decades, or in physical and spiritual explorations. At the Yoga Barn on Kimball Hill, Lisa Nigro offered yoga classes four days a week. The building now holds the Village Arts of Putney, offering classes and workshops for artists, and also the Center for Creative Healing, which helps young people and others deal with issues of bereavement.

A major arts initiative of the 1980s was the River Valley Performing Arts Center (RVPAC) housed in the former Windham College Arts Building. Not included in the sale that established Landmark College, this fine modern facility, which included a 400- and a 120-seat theatre, a dance studio, an art gallery, a large art studio, practice rooms, and numerous classrooms and offices, stood unused since the college closed in 1978. In 1985 a group of local benefactors under Ed Dodd's leadership organized the Fine Arts Building Corporation, purchased the building, and set up RVPAC as a lessee and arts organizer. For the next several years the building hummed with activity as local and nationally known performers—musicians, dancers, actors—took advantage of its superb facilities, while artists exhibited in the gallery supervised by Dorrit Merton. The list of performers included such celebrities as Isaac Stern, Lyle Lovett, Betty Carter, Tammy Wynette, and Mary Chapin Carpenter in music, Momix in dance, and a performance of *On the Waterfront* with Bud Schulberg himself directing!

Probably RVPAC's most important function was serving the community as a venue for local individuals and groups and offering the stage to local schools to enjoy performances and experience the theater first-hand. Under the direction of Jeanette Koelewyn, Putney Central students staged annual spring events that included a majority of the student body. When Jeanette passed the baton due to health problems, it took five people to replace her. For the next three years Molly Hyde and Margaret Wilson wrote plays, Peter Tavalin composed music, Virginia Scholl choreographed, and Ja-Ja Laughlin Foster designed sets. As a result of these early experiences, several Putney Central School students went on to professional careers in entertainment and others stayed active in local community theater.

Operating a large facility like RVPAC turned out to be a daunting challenge. Heating and lighting all that space, paying the small but dedicated staff, promoting and managing, all required a large cash flow. But it seemed that the more RVPAC was used the more it lost money. A variety of funding efforts were made—grants, benefits, auctions, etc.—but ultimately, after six artistically successful but financially disastrous seasons, RVPAC ceased operations. A few years later Landmark College purchased the building.

Music was always an important part of Putney's culture, from country fiddling to chamber music. The Yellow Barn Music Festival, begun in 1967, continued to thrive during the 1980s, offering a five-week summer season of almost nightly chamber music, with special events throughout the year. In the folk realm, the beloved Stockwell Brothers continued to make bluegrass music, winning ever-widening popularity while still playing local venues in Putney when the opportunity arose. Other Putney folk musicians, like Lisa McCormick, got their start in the eighties. Lisa's first album, produced by Jonathan Edwards in 1985, won three preliminary Grammy nominations. Just a few years ago, she put out her third album. Other bands, such as Tiny Monsters and Simba, have also made Putney their base of operations.

Beginning in 1981, Putney had its own local Morris dance group, led by Fred Breunig. The Putney Morris Men's colorful May Day performances at the Town Hall and elsewhere in Putney quickly became an established tradition. Other early dancers included John Smith, Alan Blood, Ian Eddy, George Carow, and Richard Ramsay. Many others performed with the group over the years, including Ken Brautigam, Darrel Daley, Jake McDermott, and musician Deb Maynard. The group's original brown bowlers and orange and yellow baldrics (crossed sashes) were replaced with red berets and red and yellow baldrics in 1990, but its distinctive dance style, with large sticks and swooping handkerchiefs remained constant. In 1985 new member Jake McDermott prodded the team into also "welcoming the May" at sunrise atop Putney Mountain. Ever since, the team has performed for an early-rising and often very chilly crowd of enthusiastic supporters who hike up the mountain on May 1 to join the celebration.

Fred Breunig's other cultural contribution in town was the revitalization of Piece's Hall in East Putney. The Hall was built in 1832 as a Methodist meeting house. After about ten years, it was sold to the Pierce family when the Methodists of East Putney and Putney combined to build a new church in town (now the Catholic Church). Community events and dances began taking place in the hall in the mid-1800s. The East Putney Community Club was first established in 1920, although the hall was still maintained privately. Thirty years later, in 1950, the deed to Pierce's Hall was given to the club by descendants of the Pierces with the stipulation that it always be used for community events. Activity at the hall has typically waxed and waned, and the mid-1970s was one of the waning periods. So when a group of dancers who lived next door to the hall approached Fred with the idea of starting a regular dance there, he was game to do it. An accomplished caller, he initiated a monthly contra and square dance that has continued to the present on the last Saturday of the month. In the mid-1980s a leak in the roof began to destroy the plaster ceiling. At that point Fred enlisted the aid of former East Putney Community Club members and more recent arrivals. In 1986, they officially incorporated the club as a Vermont non-profit organization dedicated to educational activities. During the next several years, a series of monthly potluck suppers, Halloween and Christmas parties, penny auctions, rummage sales, pancake breakfasts, and spaghetti suppers raised funds sufficient not only to repair the roof but also the historic coved (arched) plaster ceiling. In addition to dances the Hall began to be used for family reunions, rehearsals, and weddings.

SPIRITUALITY AND COMMUNITY

In the early 1980s the Church of the Brethren established a ministry in Putney. Brethren have historically been hesitant to use individual names in their writings and histories, fearing that this would lead to vanity. Out of respect for this belief, this history refers to no specific names. The Brethren bear a relationship with Quakers and the Mennonites as one of the three historic peace churches that emerged in Europe and grew from early American communities that settled in Pennsylvania. In late summer 1981, three families moved to southeastern Vermont to establish a Brethren community. They purchased a large New England farmhouse (the old Bentley house on West Hill Road), which they renovated into three separate apartments. They chose the name of Genesis for their new church, based on the account of creation found at the beginning of the Gospel of John.

The very first Brethren "love feast" was held at the newly renovated West Hill residence in October of 1981, with communion around tables, a simple meal, and washing of one another's feet as a sign of commitment to service of others. In 1984, the congregation purchased the old Stromberg home on Kimball Hill, and members began to meet there. All major decisions were to be made in unity, without taking votes. Soon after, a worship area was added to the property. Creating it was a special time for the Brethren, as many people came together to give their energy to its construction. Church members have been active in the areas of education and community service, including participation in the original working groups of Putney Family Services, Putney Cares, and the Putney Recreational League.

During the 1980s the Putney Friends Meeting increased its public presence in town through social activism and the construction of a meeting house. Spirituality is the essence of the Society of the Friends and simplicity, hospitality, and work for peace and justice are vehicles for manifesting that essence. Social activism during this time included ongoing assistance to families from Central America, participation in the Nuclear Freeze Movement, preventing domestic violence, and stopping the spread of AIDS. Under the leadership of David MacCauley of the American Friends Service Committee, Putney became the town in which the first nuclear freeze was initiated.

In 1983, Connie St. John announced her desire to make an outright gift of the Day Care Center property to Putney Friends Meeting. By this time the Friends' Meeting had begun to mature as an organization, and was in the process of attaining the stability and steady momentum that it has carried to the present time. A significant effort in establishing this stability involved the fund drive that was soon underway in earnest, to support the

Ken Pick completes the glazing process on his pottery during the Putney Holiday Crafts Tour 1990.

131

construction of the Friends' Meeting House. It was noted that the construction of the meeting house would allow tax exemption, freeing the Friends from the ethical difficulty regarding legally required taxation of property, which in part supports "participation in war." During this time the Meeting was held at The Grammar School, and then was moved to the Central School until the building was completed in November 1986.

Also significant in this period were efforts to support the rights of same-sex couples and gay and lesbian individuals. On March 15, 1987, a minute was prepared to show support for state legislation "prohibiting discrimination against lesbians and gay men in housing, jobs, custody, credit, and insurance." An oversight committee for marriage was appointed, and discussion of same-sex marriage was ongoing. On March 20, 1988, the following minute was approved:

> We affirm our willingness as a Meeting to participate in celebrations of marriage, for both opposite-sex and same-sex couples. We intend to follow the same customary and careful process of arriving at clearness for all couples who wish to unite under our care in accordance with our traditional procedures. At every step we intend to treat all couples with respect, care, and love.

In the 1980s, the Federated Church hosted many religious and non-church related groups and events, signaling passersby with a bulletin board newly installed on the front lawn. Janet Langdon, the church's first female pastor, began her tenure in February 1985. A bulletin from November 1987 shows the variety of religious and community events offered. These included a visiting Baptist minister, recognition of Jon Prentiss's compilation on Baptists in Putney, a Christmas Bazaar, a community potluck, a senior luncheon—and the meetings which have brought so many people to Putney on Wednesday evenings these past two decades—Alcoholics Anonymous, ACAP (Adult Children of Alcoholic Parents), and Al-Ateen. Also mentioned were a vigil for peace and justice in Brattleboro, an Oxfam day of fasting, and a PAP clinic and free breast exam. During that time, the church sponsored a family from El Salvador in sanctuary. The Women's Group also stitched the quilt that now hangs in Town Hall, with panels of scenes from town.

The eighties were a time of adjustment, redirection, and spiritual growth. After the stormy sixties and seventies, Putney residents took the opportunity to catch their breath and plan more soberly for the future. There was considerable relief that Landmark College had come to town. Putney's reputation as a leader in arts and education continued to grow, while its officials—the School Board, the Selectmen and the manager—worked hard to find the money to improve services and beautify the town.

9. Ending the Century: 1990s

A history of the present is the most difficult to write. Not until after the passage of time can we tell which events are long lasting and which have been a "flash in the pan." Given that the last 250 years show a trend of ups and downs, it is even harder to predict which aspects of Putney today will be important to the history of tomorrow. So, rather than analyze and attribute significance to things that may vanish with time, this final chapter will describe Putney today. Most of the information comes from the annual Town Report, responses to surveys conducted by the Putney Historical Society over the past two years, and personal interviews.

There are three events that do stand out, however, because of their larger connections: the tragic death of Judith Hart Fournier, the unexpected award of the Nobel Peace Prize to Jody Williams, and the passage of Vermont's Civil Union law. Judith Fournier, who had been a publicist for the River Valley Performing Arts Center and covered music for the *Valley Advocate*, joined the *Brattleboro Reformer* staff when RVPAC closed its doors. In 1992, she made the courageous decision to speak up for herself, and wrote a series for the newspaper about the stalking behavior of her former partner. Her personal philosophy was to do what she believed at all costs—in this case her convictions cost her her life when she was brutally murdered by her stalker. Strong attendance at candlelight vigils showed the community's deep sense of loss. As a result of support from all corners of the state, the Vermont legislature enacted a stalking bill to protect others.

Jody Williams gained attention for her international campaign against landmines and on October 14, 1997 she chose her Putney home as a backdrop for receiving the Nobel Peace Prize. Ironically, Jody was better known to the world than she was to Putney. Trying to report the "local interest" aspect of her prize, the *Brattleboro Reformer* found very few people who could identify her, although there was overwhelming support for her work. According to the International Campaign to Ban Landmines (ICBL) website:

> Jody Williams was the founding coordinator of the International Campaign to Ban Landmines (ICBL). In that capacity, she oversaw the growth of the ICBL to more than 1,300 NGOs in over eighty-five countries and served as the chief strategist and spokesperson for the campaign. Working in an unprecedented

A parade down Kimball Hill Road and onto the Common welcomed the public to the opening of Sandglass Theater in 1995. Renovation to the Tavern can be seen in the background.

cooperative effort with governments, UN bodies and the International Committee of the Red Cross, the ICBL achieved its goal of an international treaty banning antipersonnel landmines during the diplomatic conference held in Oslo in September 1997. Ms. Williams now serves as Campaign Ambassador for the ICBL, speaking on its behalf all over the world.

While Vermont Senator Patrick Leahy sponsored a bill that banned the export of land mines from the United States in 1992 and the U.S. leads the world in funding land mine clearance in other countries, it has not yet signed the international Mine Ban Treaty.

Beginning in July 2000, Vermont law offered same-sex couples the same rights as married couples. Before and after the passage of the Civil Union bill, controversy raged throughout the state, but in Putney opinion seemed generally to favor the new law. Active communities like the Friends, who stated as early as 1988 their "willingness as a Meeting to participate in celebrations of marriage, for both opposite-sex and same-sex couples" were steadfast supporters. Support came also from the United Church of Putney, the new name for the Federated Church after it dissolved the federation of Baptists, Methodists, and Congregationalists and returned to its original affiliation as a Congregational Church. The United Church of Putney became an "open and affirming" church, revising its constitution with part of the changed text reading as follows: "We believe that God's holy spirit is within all and beyond all—a spirit in whose movement there are no barriers of color, ethnicity, class, nationality, sexual orientation, gender, age, ability, or religion."

Many Putney people lobbied regarding the civil union legislation and spoke at state-level hearings in Montpelier. The legislation was helped along by support from our state representatives David Deen and Steve Darrow, and then–Senate President pro tem Peter Shumlin.

COMMUNITY WELL-BEING AND EDUCATION

An example of Putney's growing concern for social issues occurred in 1989 when Central School Principal Mike Friel called a meeting of active community volunteers like Rachel Dunham and mental health professionals such as Jacqueline Lichtenberg and Tom Ehrenberg to discuss the growing social issues that were interfering with student learning. As a result, Putney Family Services was founded in 1989 to help local families cope with the stresses of modern society. It provided thousands of hours of after school programs, summer camp scholarships, mentoring relationships, picnics, parenting workshops, and a health clinic. Its Putney Walk-in Clinic provided free healthcare to uninsured or underinsured individuals. The clinic was started in 1991 by Richard Fletcher, a nurse practitioner associated with Dr. Tom Hoskins in Putney. At first Fletcher staffed the program himself, with clerical support from another volunteer, Susan Bell. Putney Family Services provided modest funding for medical supplies and stationery, and donations from patients provided additional financial support. The clinic operated out of Tom's office (at that time, across from the Chittenden Bank). In the spring of 1996, the Clinic and Putney Family Services joined five other "free clinics" in Vermont in applying for federal grant money, which they were awarded several months later. Because of other professional and volunteer obligations, Fletcher and Bell stepped back and turned the program over to Putney Family Services, which put together a staff of volunteer health professionals (including Fletcher) and a coordinator, Elizabeth St. John. Program coordination shifted to Leon Cooper in 1998. The Clinic materialized and continues to operate today because concerned, resourceful individuals were able to work together to garner the support of the community and funding from state and federal governments.

Putney Cares's mission was boosted in 1990 when the organization was the recipient of a portion of a $99,000 Community Development Block Grant from the department of Housing and Urban Development. The funds were used to help purchase and renovate the Noyes House on Kimball Hill. (The balance of the grant was used by the town to transform the old Sheriff's office in the Town Hall to a roomy, handicapped-accessible restroom). Noyes House has provided temporary or long term shared living experiences to people in need since 1991. A barn, constructed for use by the wider community in the mid-1990s, was equipped by early 2003 with kitchen facilities and a large airy meeting room.

Center for Creative Healing was founded in 1993 by Penelope Simpson Adams and Anne Black to provide help to children effected by profound loss. The scope of CCH was later increased to address the turmoil caused by other traumatic events in the lives of children, including divorce, substance abuse, or the incarceration of a parent. The organization is based in the Yoga Barn.

Changing times and demography caused a decline in the use of the Community Center, the oldest private recreational organization in Vermont, to the point that its aging building was suffering from lack of funds and energy for needed repairs. A small and determined group led by Ian Eddy and Connie St. John revitalized the nearly 70-year-old organization in 1994 and undertook an ambitious effort to save the 110-year-old building, a former church, from further decay. Major renovations and structural repairs were slowly completed over several years including a new office wing named in honor of Ken and Shirley Ellis, who had worked tirelessly for the Center and its programs for 40 years. But even as the work was in progress, users continued to drift away. By 2001, spirits reached an all-time low and the few remaining board members began to consider dissolving the organization and giving its assets to another non-profit.

As word spread through the town grapevine, several concerned people joined the board to help save the Center and renew its mission. Rather than let the building sit unused and empty, a temporary lease was given to the Village Nursery School. Parents who brought their children to the nursery school were introduced to the building and interest and usage began to increase once again. A need for more teen social activities was recognized and the board sanctioned the revival of monthly dances for the sixth through ninth grades. Negotiations for a more permanent tenancy of the nursery school in 2002 resulted in the mutually beneficial agreement that its space would be converted for use by other community groups after school hours and that its director, Sandy Klein, would handle the scheduling of events taking place at the center.

The Community Center served as the school gym from its founding in 1925 until the present public school was built in 1958. It had once been the only place in town where kids and adults could play basketball. The Putney Central School's large gymnasium greatly reduced the need for its space, but even into the 1980s, after-school programs

The Putney Federated Church (recently renamed the United Church of Putney) underwent extensive repairs in 1991, which required the temporary removal of its steeple.

drew many kids to the Center for all sorts of games and activities. The difficulty was finding and paying a director. The Putney Recreation League was formed in 1987 with the goal of expanding recreation programs beyond the capabilities of the Community Center. Managed by a board representing a wide spectrum of townspeople, basketball, soccer, and floor hockey programs were started. Within a couple of years volleyball, youth baseball and T-ball, softball, skating, cross-country skiing, and sledding were added. Funds were raised for a colorful modern playground at the Central School, which was erected by community volunteers. The Lions Club assisted with Little League baseball, basketball, and the creation of an ice-skating rink. Many parents took turns helping with coaching and car-pooling duties. In 1991 the League took over operation of the Putney Pool from the former Recreation Club. The Putney Pool continued to be a busy spot in the summer, and in 2002, voters listened to a status report by Sarah Baker and agreed to pay a portion of the cost of rebuilding it over the next few years. In the summer of 2002, the pool became the official responsibility of the Town of Putney.

In addition to sports programs, other forms of recreation have been encouraged. Since the late 1980s, The Putney School ran summer programs in art, music, and creative writing. Early childhood programs blossomed at The Grammar School (which has also offered an award-winning summer arts program, Camp Allegro, since 1986), the Community Early Learning Center (formerly the Putney Community Day Care), Landmark College, the Putney Library, and the Community Center.

Since the mid 1990s a natural studies program called Environmental Learning for the Future has been provided for kids K–4 at the Central School under the auspices of the Vermont Institute for Natural Resources. The VINS instructor, Karen Murphy, trains volunteer parents who then work directly with the kids. Nancy Brennan and April Sargent were the original coordinators, followed by Susan Kochinskas and Tammy Severance.

Overcrowding was an issue for Putney Central as the "baby boomers" began to have their own babies. A building committee submitted a plan for an addition that would cost more than $2.5 million dollars. Even some members of the committee thought the proposal extravagant. Many citizens who were normally supportive of education mailed a plea to voters asking that they vote against the building plan. Once defeated, representatives of the "concerned citizens" met with the original building committee and some of the Central School faculty. The group discussed the space issue and when it finally came down to dollars, Lawrie Brown suggested, "We'll spend $999,999.99. And not a penny more." The next bond vote was passed and a new addition was constructed in 1993 for approximately $900,000. Volunteers helped with some of the work, like painting, to reduce costs.

In 1992, the approved school budget reached $1,582,205, and by 1995, it expanded even further to $2,042,605. The Vermont Supreme Court's Brigham decision in February 1997, declaring the state's funding of education unconstitutional, resulted in the Act 60 legislation that provoked a state-wide debate over the costs of education. While the annual discussion of the school budget at Town Meeting revealed the usual divisions, unchanged by Act 60 funding, townspeople in general have maintained their support for Putney Central School.

During the 1990s, Landmark College tripled its enrollment to nearly 400 students, and for most of the decade maintained its 3:1 teacher/student ratio. The years 1994 to 1997 were large hiring years. That growth led to the refurbishing of campus dorms, the construction of the Strauch Family Student Center, and the Click Family Sports Center, where students work with Landmark athletic pillars such as Jim Austin, Eric Evans, and John and Ellen Wood. Changes in the academic program moved from a tutorial relationship to student support through a number of learning centers at the college. Landmark also acquired the Fine Arts Building/River Valley Performing Arts Center in 1991. Although the college put much of its space to use as classrooms and office buildings, the Center's two fine theatres were refurbished and used for both student and area performances. With Landmark's funding and management the facility is becoming active again.

TOWN AFFAIRS

In the spirit of cooperation, communication, and efficiency, in May 1990 the Selectmen called Putney's first joint meeting of the School Board, the Planning Commission and the Zoning Board, the Board of Civil Authority, and the Board of Selectmen. Throughout the 1990s and into the new century, this practice has continued and expanded. The year 1990 was actually the last year that the term selectmen was officially used. At the urging of then Chairperson Jeanette White, the gender-neutral term "Selectpersons" was introduced in 1991 and by 1992 evolved to "Selectpeople" for the remainder of the decade. In the year 2001, the Town Report reflected yet another change to "Selectboard." Nine people served on the Selectboard in the past 12 years, seven of whom served at least two three-year terms: Greg Wilson, Jeanette White (who served three terms between 1988 and 1997), David Rothschild, Jeffery Shumlin, James Olivier, Douglas Harlow, and W. Andrew Robinson Jr. David Hannum Jr. and Regina Rockefeller's first terms will expire in 2004 and 2005 respectively.

The town enjoyed smooth transitions and continuity from these dedicated people who shouldered much responsibility in running the town government with all the changing laws and regulations imposed upon them. Without the assistance of town managers David Hannum Jr. (1987–1991), Shane O'Keefe (1991–1996), and Jim Mullen (1996 to present) their duties would be impossible to fulfill. Yet no one, perhaps, was more worthy of honor than the 1997 Putney Person of the Year, town clerk and treasurer Anita Coomes. The town report of 1995 noted that "because Anita Coomes keeps things in line financially, borrowing has not been necessary since 1979." Her office bulges at the seams with many years' accumulation of official town documents. One measure of the effectiveness of our town clerk could be seen in the fact that with the exception of 1987, our town report has won James P. Taylor awards from the state for merit, excellence, or outstanding achievement every single year since 1985.

The new phragmite reed bed completed in 1990 for sludge disposal from the Wastewater Treatment Facility proved to be a big disappointment. Voters approved an optimistic plan for handling waste treatment through a natural process of growing phragmite, one of the most widespread flowering plants in the world. This reed has a voracious appetite for water and finds sustenance in sludge. In addition to a lengthy lawsuit, there was much aggravation over the planned installation of a second digester that somehow doubled in cost over the original estimate. That plan was scrapped and in 1997, after trucking nine tractor-trailer loads of sludge from the facility to a landfill in northern Vermont, the reed bed was abandoned, regraded, and capped. Unable to find a local person to operate the plant, the town hired Simon Operation Services for the job. This worked out well through 1999 when Simon opted not to renew the contract. In 2000, Jon Sprague was hired to run the plant as a town employee. In March 2002 the voters were asked to approve an application for a $755,000 loan from the state for the "25 year upgrade." A new chlorine contact chamber, a second clarifier, a second rotor, and an emergency generator are included in the plans. In October 2002, Arthur Bricker, who held the job when the facility first opened in 1976, reaccepted the job of chief operator.

In 1995, the Selectboard appointed nine people to the newly-created Putney Conservation Commission. A major purpose of this commission was to devise plans for the management and protection of town-owned parcels that had been designated conservation sites. Roger Parrott, Jacquie Walker, and Pamela Cubbage served as chairpersons. The Putney Conservation Commission assisted with the mapping of trails in the Putney Central School Forest and mapped and wrote plans for the Putney Town Forest and the Bare Hill, Beatrice Aiken, and Sacketts Brook conservation sites. The most extensive work was done at the latter site (formerly called the Hi-Lo Biddy parcel), which the town acquired in 1994. In 1996 and 1997 a massive cleanup of the property was accomplished with the help of the Connecticut River Joint Commission, the Community Service Program, Putney Town Employees, and many volunteers including Earl Stockwell, whose heavy equipment removed 40,000 pounds

Sugarers gather for the Maple Sugaring contest at Harlow's Sugar House.

of trash. Each year since, more improvements have been made and the battle of the brush goes on. In 2002 Lyssa Papazian completed work on an extraordinary informational sign that includes a map of the ruins complete with photos of mill buildings that once stood on the site. The sign was placed on the site in the spring of 2003.

In addition to working with Conservation Commissions from other towns, the Putney Conservation Commission supported the efforts of the Putney Mountain Association and Westminster's Windmill Hill Pinnacle Association to complete and conserve a trail along the ridgeline, which includes the summit of Putney Mountain. In 1997, Putney's Highway Department helped the Putney Mountain Association to clean up and rebuild the Putney Mountain Trailhead. Besides offering fine views of the Green Mountains, Putney Mountain has become a major site for viewing and counting migrating hawks in the months of September and October. Seasonal averages for the past decade have included several thousand sightings of 14 different species, the most common being the broadwing hawk.

In 1998, voters at Town Meeting authorized the Selectboard to place a conservation easement on Putney Town Forest located off Putney Mountain Road through a donation of development rights to the Vermont Land Trust. A committee of concerned citizens was formed later that year to review the proposed multi-page contract and recommended that instead the town retain all rights in the land and that the Selectboard continue to hold, conserve, and manage the entire 103 acres "for the complementary purposes of recreational use and wildlife habitat protection." The 1998 article was rescinded the following year and the voters passed a new article based on the committee's recommendations.

Selling or donating development rights to preserve Putney's open lands and limit undesired growth gained support among private landowners in the past decade, with several new parcels coming under conservation easements. In 1999, the 215-acre Osgood Property off Parkman Wood Road was purchased by the Silvio Conte National Fish and Wildlife Refuge for the purpose of protecting the northern bulrush, an endangered plant found in swampy areas on the land.

In 1995 the E911 Coordinating Committee began its work on the state-mandated emergency reporting system. Many roads had to be renamed to avoid confusion caused by similar names. Sections of roads that had been cut in two, such as the eastern part of Cemetery Road in East Putney (now Pratt Road), cut off by I-91, were given new names. The western part of Hi-Lo Biddy Road became Mill Street once again because those living on the eastern section, now cut off by the closing of the stone arch bridge in 1996, objected to the proposed new name of Thwing Road (the silent "h" making it confusing to pronounce). Westminster West Road became Westminster Road and the northern section of "old Route 5" became Taylor Road. Private roads with more than one building on them were also given names. The entire town was mapped and every building was assigned a number. Much of the work was done by an outside firm but errors and omissions had to be fixed by then assistant town clerk Sharon Bice, working closely with the Post Office. This process was not completed until 1998 and not perfect for some time afterwards. In 1999, 75 new road signs were in place and having a "locatable address" was definitely a help in receiving deliveries from sources other than the Post Office. Before E911, people had to resort to making up their own numbers and posting them on their buildings in order to receive deliveries from UPS and other carriers.

BUSINESS AND SERVICES

One of the most community-minded small businesses in town is Heartstone Books. John Smith and Rosemary Ladd started selling new and used books at 67 Main Street in July 1994 and moved (with the help of many friends and neighbors) to their present location in the Putney Tavern building as soon as renovations were completed in 1996. Though discouraged by experts before they began ("Are you crazy, or independently wealthy?" and, "You'll never make it in Putney"), John and Rosemary managed to combine business survival with their desire to provide an atmosphere of community for their customers. Recently sold to Caryl Richardson, Heartstone will remain community oriented. Their neighbors in the Tavern, first the Putney Hearth Bakery and, since 2002, The Front Porch Bakery, have nicely complemented the bookstore's desire to make customers feel at home.

Everyone's Drumming manufactures West African hand drums at 4 Christian Square. Matthew Broad, originally a builder from North Salem, New York, was inspired to begin making drums after listening to Nigerian drummer Babatundi Olutungi play and speak of peace and cooperation between the world's cultures at a concert in Amherst, Massachusetts. Since 1994, Matthew and his business partner Nathaniel Hall have made and shipped their drums to music stores nationwide and through a wholesale distributor to markets in Japan, Europe, and Canada. On summer evenings in recent years, the enchanting rhythms of these drums have often filled the

Ramona Lawrence, Lillian Hill, and Andy Robinson take a stroll on the new Mabel Gray walkway.

141

air in Putney Village as a group of local drum enthusiasts stage impromptu concerts on the town common.

Camp Gone to the Dogs, founded in 1990 by Honey Loring (creator of the bumper sticker "Proud of Putney" displayed on many Putney cars) brought hundreds of campers and their canine companions from near and far to spend a week of fun and relaxation together on the campus of The Putney School from 1991 to 1997. This unusual enterprise attracted attention from national and international television programs and publications. Having outgrown local facilities, the camp is now located in Marlboro and Stowe, Vermont.

Daniel Hoviss, a carpenter from New York who studied computers to lay the groundwork for his dream of building electric cars, began Dosolutions, Inc. in 1995 and now occupies office space at 120 Main Street. The company offered advanced web-page design, general computer consulting, sales, service, repairs, programming, and upgrades to customers locally and throughout the nation. In 1996, Dosolutions programmer Albert Bupp worked with educator Fern Tavalin to develop the nation's first web-based conferencing system for sharing multimedia files and providing expert mentoring and critique to students in public schools. The model, developed for sharing music compositions, art work, historical artifacts, and literature discussions, was funded in 1995 by the U.S. Department of Education as one of 19 technology innovation challenge grants. Called The WEB Project, the program received recognition in 2000 as one of only seven programs in the United States designated by a national panel of experts as a promising practice in educational technology. Peter Tavalin, who developed the techniques used in the music composition initiative, began teaching his program at The Putney School in 1998.

When Quaker Oats closed down its plant in the former Windham College field house at 78 River Road South in the early 1990s, a new light industry took over the building. Mailrite, started by Whit Wheeler in 1987, moved to this location from Brattleboro in the late 1990s. Mailrite handles mailings for businesses, organizations, and schools, such as The Grammar School and Landmark College.

Press On, Inc. was started by John Smith in 1988 in the professional building at 125 Main Street, currently known as the Carriage House. In 1991, John was joined by partner Fred Breunig, who bought out John's share when he left the business to start Heartstone Books in 1994. Fred continued to provide Putney with personal service for all its printing, copying, and faxing needs until February 2001, when Press On merged with Doug and Sally Brown's Prospect Park Press in West Chesterfield, New Hampshire. Fortunately for Putney, the Browns kept the same neighborly atmosphere provided by John and Fred.

Opened by Jonathan Flaccus in 1976, The Unique Antique is full of old books, maps, prints, paintings, postcards, photographs, and ephemera from near and far. Jonathan's 18-room house at 71 Main Street, still also a private residence, is the former home of Seth and Margaret Ellis, who provided family living for a total of 189 children over the years, housing as many as 32 at one time. Over time there have been many other antique stores in town. One named Recollections was opened in 1998 by Indra Tracy at 118 Main Street in a building that had once been the village Texaco station.

Tavern Hill Pet Care Center was started by Putney School graduate Saskia Whallon when her planned career in gene mapping was thwarted by vision problems. Saskia has offered both grooming and boarding kennel services since 1995 at her new building at 296 River Road.

Sajen, Inc., a jewelry manufacturing enterprise owned by Marianna and Richard Jacobs, came to Putney in the early 1990s. Initially the company's small retail store, called Offerings, was located in the former Woodzels by Wetzel building at 26 Kimball Hill. In 1998 it moved to larger space on the ground floor of 10 Kimball Hill after Silver Forest of Vermont moved up the street to the old Co-op building at 14 Kimball Hill. Miraculously, the store was not seriously damaged when a raging fire destroyed the upper floors of the building on December 20, 2002.

In 1998, builders Tom and Nancy Meyer began manufacturing upscale outdoor furniture under the name of Vermont Islands. They offer tables, chairs, bar islands, and grills to customers all around the United States. Windward Performance Products is a retail and wholesale distributor of high performance parts for Audi, Volkswagen, Porsche, and American trucks. The business, started in 1990 by James McCarthy, is located in the former Sawmill Country Store building at 52 Main Street.

Charles and Kate Dodge founded Putney Mountain Winery in 1998 when they began to sell the effervescent apple wines they were creating in the basement of their home, located on the farm Kate's grandmother bought in 1941 (the site of the old Bacon farm cited at the end of Chapter 2). By September 1999 Kate and Charles were distributing their wines statewide and had opened their principal outlet and tasting room at Basketville in the village of Putney. The winery's mission is to make delicious fruit wine using the best available local produce. As of 2003 the winery is making effervescent apple wines (both bulk carbonated and methode champenoise) and still wines from a variety of local

This trickster runs an obstacle at Camp Gone to the Dogs, held on The Putney School Campus in the mid-1990s.

143

Every fall hawk watchers trek to the top of Putney Mountain to count the number of birds migrating south.

produce including apples, rhubarb, blueberries, and black currants. The winery also makes an apple liqueur, Putney Pommeau, by blending together heirloom apple juice with apple brandy distilled from the winery's own heirloom apple wine.

Oak Meadow, Inc. is a business, but also a school without walls. Lawrence and Bonnie Williams started Oak Meadow in Ojai, California in 1975 and moved to Putney in 1996. Their offices are located on the second floor of the Putney Tavern building with additional space in the Carriage House. Oak Meadow employs about 25 people, including 15 teachers, and supplies teaching materials and support to charter schools and home-based students.

With the exception of Mellen's, the same convenience stores that existed in 1953 are still in business in 2003. Dwight Smith's grocery store and filling station became Sam's Market and, since 1979, Mountain Paul's General Store. The Putney General Store was purchased from the Fairchild family by Dan Mitnik and Shari Gliedman in 2000 but no changes were made in the store's line or friendly atmosphere. Shari's initial introduction to Putney was as a Windham College student. Recently, she has been involved in organizing the Southern Vermont Equine Rescue in Putney, "helping down-on-their-luck horses gain a second chance in life." Shari and co-founder Laurie Bayer were "horse people who saw the need to help . . . as many of these noble animals as [they can, preventing them] from heading down a long, unforgiving road to a slaughter house."

The Putney Consumers Cooperative, known as "The Co-op," moved to its beautiful new building at 8 Carol Brown Way in 1992, and continued to offer quality organic foods and produce as well as general groceries. In keeping with the emphasis on healthy food alternatives, it stopped selling cigarettes in 1996.

144

Putney's dining establishments offer a variety of choices. The Putney Inn, though relaxed and casual, is approaching its 40th year of offering excellent cuisine to the general public and catering to many private parties, weddings, and conferences. The Putney Diner, located at 128 Main Street since 1992, is owned by Deb Julian and managed by Karen Zamojski. Karen's pies won the Diner a recommendation from *USA Today* as one of the ten best places in the United States to eat. Waitress Ellie Lascore, who not only doesn't write down your order but also remembers your preferences on your next visit, was named Putney's Person of the Year in 2002. Next door to the diner is the Putney Village Pizza, owned and operated by John Papadopoulos since 1994. In addition to all these options, the three grocery stores each has its own snack bar.

During the warmer months, people have been known to drive from far away places with cravings for the chicken or ribs at Curtis' All American B-B-Q, and since 1991, from May until November, Bert Wilkins is ready to serve hot dogs, hamburgers, and other specialities from Bert's Chuck Wagon at 63 Main Street. A flower garden and small fountain provide atmosphere for enjoying a meal at picnic tables shared with friends and neighbors.

The Gulf station on Main Street, operated by Tom Hayes as Main Street Service Center from 1984, became Main Street Repair, run by Dennis Bailey in 2001. In March 2002, Tom opened Tom's Auto Repair and Small Engine Service in a new garage at his home at 22 Hickory Ridge Road South. Greg Winchester joined his father Rodney at Rod's Mobil, offering gas, towing, and repair. Ron Holway and Ray Fortier ran an auto body business at 4 Christian Square in the 1970s, but subsequently Ron has done auto body and repair work under the name of West Hill Auto Body at 158 Aiken Road. Ray opened a shop near his home on Houghton Brook Road before moving it to Ray Fortier's Auto Body at 76 River Road South.

Bellows Falls Trust became Chittenden Bank in 1993. The Putney Credit Union moved from its tiny building at 97 Main Street to a roomier location at 79 Main Street in the early 1990s. In 1998, because it had come to serve far more than just the town of Putney, its name was changed to River Valley Credit Union. Of course both the bank and the credit union have a drive-up ATM.

Travelers looking for accommodations in Putney can choose between the Putney Inn's motel and two B&Bs, Hickory Ridge and the Copper Kettle. On crowded holiday and foliage weekends, the Brattleboro Chamber of Commerce makes arrangements to place some of the overflow of travelers in private homes. In early fall The Grammar School's colorful Medieval Faire attracts huge crowds, and on Columbus Day weekend, the combination of peak foliage and Putney School's Harvest Festival make Putney a favorite place to visit.

Derrig Excavating, Green Mountain Well, and Temple Plumbing are as busy as ever after more than four decades of service, the businesses passing from one generation to the next. Susan Heller, new owner of Mimi Oriental Products, originally founded by Hi Kyung Brandt, is still making delicious egg rolls.

Additionally, numerous service providers find Putney to be fertile soil for private practice. During the 1990s several psychotherapy offices opened in town, including Mareka Ohlson, providing services since December of 1993; Patty Krasner, since November of 1996; and Barry Shaw, since July of 1997. New physical therapists in town include Priscilla Svec and Todd Miller, grandson of the late Putney farmer Ellwyn Miller. Also new to the landscape are offices for massage therapy, including those of Deb Berigow and Lisa Johndrow. Lisa Nigro offers yoga classes four days per week at The Yoga Barn on 114 Westminster Road. The Village Arts of Putney, also located in the Yoga Barn, offers workshops to artists and classes for aspiring artists.

In spite of general growth and expansion of services, things change and eras come to an end. The Putney Summit restaurant at 109 Bellows Falls Road, run by the Narkiewicz family for nearly 20 years, shut its doors in 2001. Lawrence Cook and Judith Morton retired in 2002, closing Cook and Morton Realty, Putney's handy real estate office for the last 30 years. When Richard and Susanna Ramsey decided to return to Mexico in 1998, Putney lost its first and only authentic Mexican Restaurant, Casa del Sol, which was located at 64 Main Street. However, typical of Putney, it was shortly replaced with a successful catering business, Elizabethan Fare.

VILLAGE IMPROVEMENTS

One of the goals of the Selectboard at the beginning of the 1990s was the gradual revitalization of downtown Putney and one of the major projects undertaken was the Mabel Gray Walkway. Mabel was the much-loved, long-term resident who requested at the 1983 Town Meeting, and at every subsequent meeting, that the town build a sidewalk from the

Over 300 people turned out for the first annual town picnic in September 2002 and enjoyed a potluck luncheon, music, games, and each others' company.

village to the Putney Central School so that children could walk safely to and from school. The first recorded mention of the idea was by Inez Harlow in 1952, who "suggested that some sort of sidewalk be built on Kimball Hill . . . especially for the benefit of the school children." The cost was estimated at $200,000 to $300,000, and in 1992 the town applied for grants for 90 percent of that amount, the balance to be raised locally. Landowners donated 43 easements along the 1-mile route. Energetic fundraising raised $28,000 by 1995, but delays in the design and construction plans, which were the responsibility of the Vermont Agency of Transportation, kept delaying the start date and increasing the costs. Active support from legislators resolved the impasse by transferring the authority to proceed to the town. Other costs not included in the original estimate were $33,000 for 4,400 cubic feet of hand-laid stone walls and $61,500 for 2,460 linear feet of granite curb. The Walkway was finally completed in 1998, at a total cost of $600,000, three times the lower estimate presented at Town Meeting in 1992, but nonetheless a great improvement to the town's infrastructure. This experience caused understandable skepticism about the proposed cost of any major project ever since. A book was put together and donated to the Putney Historical Society by Thera Hindmarsh that documents the whole story. In 2001, Robert Hindmarsh was named Honorary Superintendent of the Mabel Gray Walkway.

In the process of developing the new Walkway, a plan to change the intersection of Route 5 and the "Kimball Hill" section of Westminster West Road was implemented for safety reasons and to increase the area of the Town Green. It was hoped that the practice of just slowing down a bit to make the turn onto Route 5 would cease with the new "T" design. But in reality, it took the persistent efforts of a deputy sheriff and some very hefty fines to convince people that a complete stop was required, "or else."

Putney Paper mounted a large remodeling effort that changed the southern side of the main building, greatly reducing noise coming from the machines and creating an attractive new entrance complete with a small lawn. In 1991, the Federated Church had a Sesquicentennial restoration, which involved, among other things, refurbishing its steeple and taking down a large tree on its front lawn. Several private homes in the village were renovated inside and out, including the former private residence at 126 Main Street now occupied by Dr. Tom Hoskins's Putney Medical Office and by Mareka Ohlson, psychotherapist. Dr. Hoskins was named Putney Person of the Year in 2001, his 21st year in practice in Putney.

The most noticeable and appreciated improvement of all was the reincarnation of the derelict Putney Tavern building. Peter and Deb Shumlin purchased the property at a public auction in 1995 and immediately began restoring it to its original lines, including the addition of its original grand porch. Tim Severance Builders did the construction. The large crowd of people attending the open house in 1996 was thrilled with the transformation, inside and out. Oak Meadow, Heartstone Books, and the Putney Hearth Bakery moved into the completed building, enlivening the center of town immeasurably. The Shumlins also purchased and renovated the one-story building behind the Town Hall, adding two floors to create the Carriage House. The second floor contains professional space, and the third floor apartments, while Press On and the laundromat Martha's Washtub continued to occupy the ground floor. Craig and Elizabeth Stead owned and operated the laundromat since the 1960s, and though the Shumlins kept it open for awhile, they eventually made the decision to close it, in the belief that the amount of water it used was lowering the town's water table. Many people protested the closing to no avail.

In 2000, a remodeling project on the lower floor of the Town Hall created a new office for the town treasurer to relieve some of the space problems. In the process, a temporary office was constructed for the Putney Historical Society, which gave up some of its museum space and moved many artifacts and display cases to the stage area upstairs in the Town Hall. The listers, whose space requirements had likewise been steadily increasing, are also in need of an office of their own. Long range plans for the Town Hall include more remodeling on the ground floor, repair or replacement of the leaking roof and possibly, someday, an elevator to provide handicap-access to the large meeting hall on the second floor, where Town Meeting was held from about 1872 until 1985. The only public event held there in the 1990s was the annual Putney Artists' Exhibit (first started in 1994 to benefit the Mabel Gray Walkway fund) from July into October. In 1996, the exterior of the building was painted in its original color and, thanks to Lola Aiken, Milly Ellis, and Rod Payne-Meyer, major improvements were done on the gardens on the east and south sides of the building.

Main Street was once lined with large trees, now long gone. Unfortunately, due to problems with roots from large trees interfering with sidewalks, power lines, and sewer systems, the canopied effect of a century ago cannot be recreated. But in 2002, after two years of preparation and with the help of private donations and a grant from the Urban and Community Forestry Program, commission members planted eight trees at various appropriate locations along Main Street. Most of the planting was done during a snow storm on May 18!

Not all improvements have been purely physical. The establishment of Sandglass Theater on Kimball Hill Road in 1995 has brought artistic and spiritual gifts to Putney. Eric Bass and Ines Zeller-Bass, world-renowned puppeteers, transformed the S.L. Davis

Putney School's tradition of cross-country skiing continues each year with the Putney Relays.

horse stable behind the Federated Church into an intimate 60-seat puppet theater. Eric and Ines produce original works and offer two touring repertoires, one for adults and one for young audiences. The Sandglass company creates new puppets for each show to correspond with a particular piece and the precise metaphor they are trying to achieve. In addition to their own shows, Sandglass presents the works of other outstanding international theater artists as well and sponsors an international puppet festival every other year called Puppets in the Green Mountains.

Inspired by a refurbished upstairs at Town Hall, Linn Bruce decided to organize a show for area professional artists. The show calls attention to the town of Putney as a center for artists. Expanding on Linn's original efforts, an exhibit continues each year from early August until mid-October.

STYLE OF LIVING

According to census records, by 2000 there were 2,634 people calling Putney home—a 12 percent increase since 1990, and a 250 percent increase over the past century. Of that number, 1,404 were employed persons aged 16 or over, 33 percent of whom worked in the educational, health, and social services field; 14.6 percent of whom were self-employed (in non-incorporated businesses); and 11.4 percent of whom were government workers. Most notable among the remaining classifications of occupations was agriculture (combined with forestry, fishing, hunting, and mining as one category), which had shrunk to just 2.4 percent of Putney's workforce. A section of the census dealing with "commuting to work" listed 93 people working at home in 2000 and 118 walking to work. 174 people reported carpooling while 972 "drove alone."

Comments from a Putney Historical Society survey distributed in 2002 give a more personal view of who lives in town and why:

> On a workday I get up before 6 am. I enjoy and admire the colors of sunrise and the wildlife in my yard. I work in a neighboring town and arrive home by dinnertime. Days off include a long walk in the neighborhood. . . . When the peace, serenity, and solitude at home become unbearable, I'll go to town to recycle, pick up mail, hit the bookstore, get some bread at the bakery, and pick up items at the Coop. I have strong hermit tendencies and one of the things I love about Putney is that a trip to buy groceries usually includes a number of social opportunities.

> Putney feels like a community, not just a town. I love Putney and try to do as much business and buying here as I can.

> My sister lives in Florida. I sent her a birthday card and an old photo and a self-addressed-stamped envelope so that she could write back. I then hurried off to a computer class on Saturday morning. On the way, I realized I forgot the stamp on the inner envelope and forgot to seal the outer one. I stopped in Harmonyville and called the Post Office. And they fished it out, put the stamp

on, and sealed it. Only in Putney!

Each morning I gaze out the window overlooking the Great Meadows and across the Connecticut River to New Hampshire. . . . I remember one morning looking out and seeing patches of snow covering the ground. I watched in amazement as those white patches swirled and rose in the air! It was my first sighting of the snow geese who make the Great Meadows a stopping place on their migration route.

We moved up to Putney in 1970. I was attracted to the town and the burgeoning of "new" ideas. . . . I found out after I moved here that I was descended by about five generations from Benjamin Bellows after whom the nearby town of Bellows Falls was named.

I was born in Putney and have lived here most of my years. My grandfather Austin delivered ice around town and there is a picture in Town Hall of him and his sons delivering ice. . . . I just like living in Putney and seeing old and new friends and watching good things happen, like the recreation pool and all the sports activities that my grankids are involved in.

My close friend from college grew up in Putney and asked a few of us (friends from college) to move to southern Vermont after we graduated. I discovered that I love the small town feel and openness of Putney. We have lived in Halifax and East Dummerston, but I am always drawn back to Putney.

I was a student in the Master of Arts in Teaching English as a Second Language program at the School for International Training in 1978 and met my current partner in life there. Other than 9 months teaching elsewhere, I've been living in Putney ever since.

I moved to Putney because the price of land was cheaper here than in West Brattleboro, Guilford, or Marlboro and my husband and I wanted a place to settle down and raise children. I telecommute. So, early in the morning I get up and check my e-mail. From there, I either write or travel to meetings in northern Vermont or other parts of the country. I love the freedom of setting my own schedule and enjoy the clean air, good water, and contact with my friends.

I was born here. I feel like I am a full citizen of the town and landscape, like I own it collectively, belong here, and am from here. I stay here because the land is lovely, there are all sorts of activist groups, creative businesses, experimental buildings and technology, working farms, and a culture of learning.

I've been a farmer all my life. My parents and ancestors came to Putney from 1840 and before. It's the best place on earth. On a recent Sunday trip to

Connecticut I was so thankful of being a Putney resident that I could hardly contain myself!!

The Washburn/Goodell family has farmed in Putney since the early to mid 1800s. Bob Goodell, born in 1918, great-grandson of Asa Washburn, has been farming at Dellside Farm (also known as the Washburn Farm) since his childhood. Bob's sons Robert and Clayton, born in 1943 and 1951, have been doing the same, running tractors since they were seven or eight years old. Daughter Jill keeps the books and is financial manager. Bob's wife Rowena Loomis came from a farm family as well. Her father and his brothers owned the largest part of the Great Meadows until the mid-twentieth century. The land has been recently re-acquired by the family. As Bob recounts, "I was never so happy as when my children acquired part of the Great Meadows back again in the mid-1990s." Today the Westminster Farms and Dellside Farm make up one of the largest dairy farm operations in Vermont, producing 10 million pounds of milk per year. Bob's three grandsons attended "the college of hard knocks" and went directly from high school to work on the farm alongside their parents. Four granddaughters, still in school, help out when the occasion arises.

Ironically, though the number of farms has dwindled, the overall number of farm animals and crop yields has risen. Though they aren't swimming the river to pasture

Jim Powers of the Brattleboro Reformer *took this photo of the fire that claimed the barn at the Colan Johnson pig farm on Pratt Road in the 1990s.*

in Westmoreland, New Hampshire any more, you can still find livestock out on River Road, including Holsteins and sheep. In January and February in the 1990s, John Nopper of River View Farm had something over 150 ewes lambing, with maybe two or three lambs each. Though the bottom has dropped out of the wool market, the young are sold for meat and more recently for their blood, which is processed to obtain antibodies for medical use.

Harlow's and Green Mountain Orchards continue to raise tasty apples and berries, with popular pick-your-own periods every summer and fall. Wilson's Tree Farm offers Christmas trees to cut and wreaths and greens by mail order. Clearly the nature of agriculture in Vermont had changed, and traditional operations had to change with it, through upgrading facilities and seeking new markets related to new technology, an upscale clientele, or tourism.

With an increase in population has come a shortage in affordable housing. Putney Meadows, a much-needed housing project, was completed in 1993 to provide efficiency apartments for elderly or otherwise qualified residents. In 1996, a $268,480 grant was received from the Vermont Community Development Program enabling the Brattleboro Area Community Land Trust to purchase and manage the former Germon's Mobile Home Park. Extensive upgrades were made throughout the park, which was renamed Locust Hill Mobil Home Park.

Residents of McAllister's Mobil Home Park were not as fortunate. The McAllisters were unable to find a buyer and other efforts to keep the park viable bore no fruit. When it closed for good in 2002, many of the long-term residents faced financial losses and personal hardship. Thanks to a state grant administered by the Rockingham Trust, some residents did receive some relocation assistance. Some residents got no help.

A revolving loan fund managed by the Windham Regional Commission assists qualified people in need of housing improvements that involve health and safety problems. Funding sources originally came in 1996 from the Vermont Community Development Program for $200,500 and several private contributions, along with amounts from Putney's White/Whitney and Edwald Funds.

EPILOGUE

For many decades Putney youth have left town to seek the wider opportunities available elsewhere. Since the 1940s their numbers have been more than replaced by the influx of new people who have had their fill of city life and the corporate rat race. Attracted to the way of life they experienced here through their connections to the Experiment, Putney School, and Windham College, many "new-comers" are now long-term residents of 25–60 years. Newer layers of immigration to town have been prompted by the availability of land from the 1960s through the 1980s, a growing arts community, and most recently, home schooling and the town's liberal acceptance of its gay population. Life is still slower here, dress is always casual, there is no closed, pretentious society, and there are increasingly more and varied cultural activities to satisfy most anyone. The main consideration for those who wish to live here is the cost and availability of real estate.

The biggest loss to the town elders is the sense that everyone knows everyone else. In an attempt to recreate that sense of knowing your neighbors, John Caldwell, with the help of a committee he enlisted, coordinated the first annual Putney Town Picnic, held on September 7, 2002 on the grounds of Putney Central School. It was a smashing success. Though free to all who came, everyone was requested to bring a potluck dish to share, the result of which was a tantalizing array of far more choices than one could possibly sample. Hot dogs, hamburgers, apples, and soft drinks were provided courtesy of several local businesses that donated generously to promote this uniting endeavor. An estimated 400 residents of the town spent some portion of the day there. Pianist Peter Tavalin and violinist Katie Graves provided music, with Eric Lawrence sitting in for a few tunes on sax. Peter Graves, renowned sportscaster, emceed. Polly Washburn coordinated games and attractions for the kids. The Fire Department brought a fire truck for the kids to climb on. Steve Ingram and Mike Mrowicki transported tables, chairs, signs, and trash. Everyone agreed that this should be an annual event.

The workers at the Basket Shop have long since retired: Basketville now employs only retail and office workers. The Putney Nursery, employer of varying numbers of people since the 1920s, ceased in the late 1990s. Santa's Land, which in its peak years during the 1970s and 1980s had as many as 50 people on the payroll, is operating on a part-time, limited basis. At Putney Paper there are just a few workers left who have spent their entire careers there. Even so, they employ about 150 people who make 67 tons of paper a day from 100 percent recycled materials. With the exception of

Landmark College, there are no new companies employing any sizeable percentage of Putney's people.

On a brisk autumn day, a walker on Putney's dirt roads may have the Putney biking team flash by, be passed by joggers from Landmark, overtaken by horses, or stop to view the very occasional moose. Seasonal events, such as May Day dancing, the Yellow Barn concerts, the Putney Area Artists Show, Harvest Festival, the Medieval Faire, the Green Mountain Head, the Putney Crafts Tour, and a growing, family-oriented turnout of costumed characters in the village on Halloween offer colorful punctuation marks for the changing seasons. Putney, more than ever before, is a busy town of colorful expression.

As we head toward the 250th anniversary of the town's charter, there is much to consider and many important choices yet to be made. We are asking questions about how to maintain a viable economy that includes agriculture, what to do about our open land, what sources of fuel and electricity to pursue, how both to honor the past and welcome the future.

As the people of Putney, along with every other community in the nation, have been forced in recent years to face vast and menacing problems far beyond the everyday cares of small town life, local disagreements have become trivial and global concerns have bound everyone to the common desire for peace and understanding between the world's disparate cultures. As the world has changed, our lives go on and the desire to leave our children with a better place to live is unchanged.

Putney village was a much quieter place in the early twentieth century when snow stopped all automobile travel and town looked more like this late 1800s photo. Louisa Amidon, who has lived in her Putney home for most of the twentieth century, remembers falling asleep as a small child to the tinkling sounds of sleigh bells as horses passed by on the road.

BIBLIOGRAPHY

Andrews, Ed & Crawford, David. Correspondence between 1837–1851. On file at the Putney Historical Society.

Andrews, Elisha. "An Historical Sermon Delivered by the Rev. Elisha D. Andrews: Fast Day, April 8, 1925." Copied from the notebooks of Clifford Cory by J. Shaaf for the Hickory Ridge School, Putney, April 1949. On file at the Putney Historical Society.

Arms, Jane. *The Putney School Aborning*. Putney, Vermont: Jane Arms, 1959.

Bacon, Justin Homer. "Notes to Posterity." Unpublished, 1961. On file at the Putney Historical Society.

Brattleboro Reformer:

"Picturesque Putney." Supplement, August 1901.

"Four Drown as Ferry Boat With Two Autos Sinks to River Bed" August 19, 1930, reprinted April 26, 1988, page 8.

"Putney Driver Loses Gas Ration." April 21, 1941.

March 21, 1943. Advertisements.

"Edwin Smith to Teach at Putney School." March 6, 1949.

"New Link of Interstate to Open." December 7, 1961.

"School Board Conflict with Putney Teachers." March 10, 1966.

March 12–June 18, 1966. Letters to the editor.

"Paul Grout to Become Denominational Moderator for Church of the Brethren." October 28–29, 2000, page 13.

Burns, Charles. Press release. August 2, 1953.

Cooke, Beverly. "Reflections on Number 7 School, East Putney, Vermont." Unpublished paper, 1994. On file at the Putney Historical Society.

"Chronological Supplement." West River Mission Visitors' Report, 1987, page 6. On file at the Putney Historical Society.

Ellis, Russell. "The Experiment in International Living." Unpublished paper, 2001. On file at the Putney Historical Society.

Ewald, J. Richard with Adair Mulligan. *Proud to Live Here: In the Connecticut River Valley of Vermont and New Hampshire*. Charlestown, NH: Connecticut River Joint Commissions, 2003.

"Recover Two of Four Putney Ferry Victims" *Claremont Daily Eagle*, August 19, 1930, reprinted in *The Walpole Gazette*, January 8, 1988, page 19.

Frazer, Kay. "Putney Friends Meeting — 1989–2002." Summary of minutes from Putney

Friends Meeting, 2002. On file at the Putney Historical Society.

Gallagher, Nancy. *Breeding Better Vermonters: The Eugenics Project in the Green Mountain State*. Hanover, NH: University Press of New England, 1999.

Greenwood, Eva D. *Personal War Sketches: Grand Army of the Republic*. Presented to the Colonel W.H. Greenwood Post No. 90, Putney. Philadelphia, PA: L.H. Everts, 1890.

Landmark College website (www.landmark.edu). Visited September 9, 2002.

"Learning from Elders." Audio and video interviews collected by seventh and eighth grade students of Fern Tavalin at Putney Central School from 1987–1991. In collection of the Putney Historical Society.

Lloyd, Susan. *The Putney School: A Progressive Experiment*. New Haven, CT: Yale University Press, 1987.

"Official Valley League Score Book, 1934–1935." In collection of Quinton Carr.

Owen, Monica, Jr. "A Study of the Town of Putney, Vermont." Student term paper at Putney School, 1936. On file at the Putney Historical Society.

Papazian, Lyssa. "A History of the Houghton Farm, Putney, VT." In *Conservation Techniques for Historic Structures*. In collection of the Putney Historical Society.

Plowden, David. *Small Town America*. New York: Harry N. Abrams, 1994.

Putney Center Reporter. 1943–1945. Bi-weekly newsletter. Collection on file at the Putney Historical Society.

"Putney Information Booklet." Prepared by Putney Community Group, 1994.

Putney Neighbors. Weekly newsletter written and printed by Jordan D. Cole, 1972–1977. Collection on file at the Putney Historical Society.

Putney News. Weekly newsletter written and printed by Dwight Smith, 1948–1956. Collection on file at the Putney Historical Society.

Putney Pamphleteer. Monthly newsletter published by seventh and eighth grade class at Putney Central from 1989–1994. On file at the Putney Historical Society.

Putney: 1753–1953. Edith De Wolfe, Laura H. Frost, Edith I. Gassett, Inez S. Harlow, Elizabeth G. Scott, eds. Putney: Fortnightly Club of Putney, 1953.

Putney Town Records, 1760–2002.

"Putney 2003." Collection of video interviews and written notes conducted under auspices of the Putney Historical Society for Celebration 2003. Funded by the Vermont Council on the Humanities. 2002–2003. On file at the Putney Historical Society (interview summaries available online at www.putneyvt.org/history/).

Putney, Vermont website (www.putney.net). Visited February 20, 2003.

Sherman, Joe. *Fast Lane on a Dirt Road: A Contemporary History of Vermont*. White River Junction, VT: Chelsea Green, 2000.

Southern Vermont Equine Rescue website (www.kenwoodfarms.com/sver/). Visited February 20, 2003.

Stockwell, Shirley. "Putney Paper 1938–1984." Laurel Ellis, ed. Unpublished paper. On file at the Putney Historical Society.

"A Summary Outline of Minutes of Friends Meeting: 1964–1988." Prepared by Recording Clerk Kay Frazer, 2000. On file at the Putney Historical Society.

Thomas, Robert M. "Edwin S. Smith, One of the First N.L.R.B. Officials: Backer of Soviet Amity." *New York Times*, November 30, 1976.

Treat, Mary Lou, and Mills, Elizabeth. "Carol 'Hutch' Maynard." Unpublished paper, 2002. On file at the Putney Historical Society.

Turbak, Gary. "Death March Across Germany." *VFW Magazine*, December 1999.

"Twentieth Century Memories: Putney, Vermont." Audio collection of Putney Historical Society lectures and oral history interviews from 1953 to 1999. Mastered to CD by Bill Shaw. Brattleboro, VT: Soundesign Recording Studio, 2002.

The United Church of Putney records. In possession of church clerk.

The United States Census Reports, 1850–2000.

"Vermont Historic Preservation Plan: Agriculture Theme." Montpelier: Vermont Division for Historic Preservation, 1990.

Watt, Donald. *Intelligence is Not Enough*. Putney: The Experiment Press, 1967.

Wheeler, Scott. *Rumrunners and Revenuers: Prohibition in Vermont*. Shelburne, VT: New England Press, 2002.

Wilson, Frank G. *Basketville: the Autobiography of Frank G. Wilson*. New York: Vantage Press, 1990.

Beatrice Aiken displays a cake at the 200th birthday celebration dinner held at Putney's Federated Church.

INDEX

In 1953 townspeople filled the center of Putney to celebrate the 200th anniversary of the signing of its first charter.

www.ingramcontent.com/pod-product-compliance
Lightning Source LLC
Chambersburg PA
CBHW050616110426
42813CB00008B/2581

* 9 7 8 1 5 8 9 7 3 1 6 2 2 *